# Apostolic Succession in an Ecumenical Context

# Apostolic Succession in an Ecumenical Context

## THOMAS M. KOCIK

ALBA·HOUSE    NEW·YORK

SOCIETY OF ST. PAUL, 2187 VICTORY BLVD., STATEN ISLAND, NEW YORK 10314

Library of Congress Cataloging-in-Publication Data

Kocik, Thomas M.
    Apostolic succession in an ecumenical context / Thomas M. Kocik.
        p.      cm.
    Includes bibliographical references.
    ISBN 0-8189-0759-2
    1. Apostolic succession — History of doctrines. 2. Tradition
(Theology) — History of doctrines. 3. Episcopacy. 4 Ecumenical
movement — History.  I. Title.
    BV665.K68      1996
    262'.11 — dc20                              96-17191
                                                CIP

Produced and designed in the United States of America by the
Fathers and Brothers of the Society of St. Paul,
2187 Victory Boulevard, Staten Island, New York 10314,
as part of their communications apostolate.


ISBN: 0-8189-0759-2

**Printing Information:**

Current Printing - first digit      1    2    3    4    5    6    7    8    9    10

Year of Current Printing - first year shown

1996          1997          1998          1999          2000          2001

*To the Immaculate ever-Virgin Mary,*
*Queen of Apostles and Mother of the Church,*
*who prays unceasingly for the unity of*
*her Son's disciples*

# Table of Contents

# Biblical Abbreviations

## OLD TESTAMENT

| | | | | | |
|---|---|---|---|---|---|
| Genesis | Gn | Nehemiah | Ne | Baruch | Ba |
| Exodus | Ex | Tobit | Tb | Ezekiel | Ezk |
| Leviticus | Lv | Judith | Jdt | Daniel | Dn |
| Numbers | Nb | Esther | Est | Hosea | Ho |
| Deuteronomy | Dt | 1 Maccabees | 1 M | Joel | Jl |
| Joshua | Jos | 2 Maccabees | 2 M | Amos | Am |
| Judges | Jg | Job | Jb | Obadiah | Ob |
| Ruth | Rt | Psalms | Ps | Jonah | Jon |
| 1 Samuel | 1 S | Proverbs | Pr | Micah | Mi |
| 2 Samuel | 2 S | Ecclesiastes | Ec | Nahum | Na |
| 1 Kings | 1 K | Song of Songs | Sg | Habakkuk | Hab |
| 2 Kings | 2 K | Wisdom | Ws | Zephaniah | Zp |
| 1 Chronicles | 1 Ch | Sirach | Si | Haggai | Hg |
| 2 Chronicles | 2 Ch | Isaiah | Is | Malachi | Ml |
| Ezra | Ezr | Jeremiah | Jr | Zechariah | Zc |
| | | Lamentations | Lm | | |

## NEW TESTAMENT

| | | | | | |
|---|---|---|---|---|---|
| Matthew | Mt | Ephesians | Eph | Hebrews | Heb |
| Mark | Mk | Philippians | Ph | James | Jm |
| Luke | Lk | Colossians | Col | 1 Peter | 1 P |
| John | Jn | 1 Thessalonians | 1 Th | 2 Peter | 2 P |
| Acts | Ac | 2 Thessalonians | 2 Th | 1 John | 1 Jn |
| Romans | Rm | 1 Timothy | 1 Tm | 2 John | 2 Jn |
| 1 Corinthians | 1 Cor | 2 Timothy | 2 Tm | 3 John | 3 Jn |
| 2 Corinthians | 2 Cor | Titus | Tt | Jude | Jude |
| Galatians | Gal | Philemon | Phm | Revelation | Rv |

# Abbreviations

CCC   *Catechism of the Catholic Church.* Ignatius Press - Libreria
Editrice Vaticana, 1994.

CD    Vatican Council II, Decree on the Pastoral Office of Bishops in
the Church (*Christus Dominus*), 1965.

DS    Henricus Denzinger and Adolfus Schönmetzer, SJ, eds.,
*Enchiridion Symbolorum, Definitionum et Declarationum de rebus
Fidei et Morum*, 34th ed. Barcelona: Herder, 1967.

DV    Vatican Council II, Dogmatic Constitution on Divine Revelation (*Dei Verbum*), 1965.

GiA   *Growth in Agreement. Reports and Agreed Statements of Ecumenical Conversations at World Level,* ed. Harding Meyer and Lukas
Vischer. New York: Paulist Press; Geneva: W.C.C., 1984.

ITC   *International Theological Commission: Texts and Documents,
1969-1985,* ed. Rev. Michael Sharkey, with a Foreword by
Joseph Cardinal Ratzinger. San Francisco: Ignatius Press, 1989.

LG    Vatican Council II, Dogmatic Constitution on the Church
(*Lumen Gentium*), 1964.

OE    Vatican Council II, Decree on the Catholic Eastern Churches
(*Orientalium Ecclesiarum*), 1964.

PCT   Joseph Cardinal Ratzinger, *Principles of Catholic Theology:
Building Stones for a Fundamental Theology,* trans. Sister Mary
Frances McCarthy, SND. San Francisco: Ignatius Press, 1987.

PG    *Patrologia Græca,* ed. J.P. Migne, 162 vols. Paris, 1857 ff.

PL    *Patrologia Latina,* ed. J.P. Migne, 217 vols. + 4 index vols.
Paris, 1844 ff.

PO    Vatican Council II, Decree on the Ministry and Life of Priests
(*Presbyterorum Ordinis*), 1965.

TCT   John F. Clarkson, SJ, et al., eds., *The Church Teaches: Documents
of the Church in English Translation.* B. Herder Book Co., 1955;
reprint, Rockford, IL: TAN Books and Publishers, 1973.

UR     Vatican Council II, Decree on Ecumenism (*Unitatis Redintegratio*), 1964.

UUS    Pope John Paul II, Encyclical "On Commitment to Ecumenism," *Ut Unum Sint*, May 25, 1995.


All biblical quotations are from the Revised Standard Version (Catholic edition).

Quotations from the documents of Vatican II are taken from Austin Flannery, OP, gen. ed., *Vatican Council II. The Conciliar and Post Conciliar Documents*, rev. ed., Vatican Collection Series (Northport, NY: Costello Publishing Company, 1988).

# Preface

In the Fall of 1991, early in my seminary years, I attended a lecture given by the renowned German theologian Bishop Walter Kasper. His presentation was entitled "Apostolic Succession in Episcopacy in an Ecumenical Context." Because of my interest in ecclesiology — the study of the mystery of the Church — I thought it worthwhile to learn what contemporary theologians are saying about that which the Catholic Church has always prized as the mark of her authenticity: her historical continuity, through the apostolic succession of bishops, with the apostolic Church of the New Testament. Bishop Kasper spoke of the need to situate the apostolic succession in a broader context. At the time — or at least until I read carefully the text of his lecture — I supposed this was an attempt, made in the interest of ecumenism, to "soften" the Catholic Church's position on the invalidity of Order and sacraments in Protestantism, which lacks the historical episcopate. But this was not the case. It later occurred to me that Bishop Kasper was recapitulating what Cardinal Ratzinger had said some years earlier, namely, that Tradition and the apostolic succession together constitute the chief ecumenical issue in the Catholic-Reformed dispute, precisely because it relates directly to the nature of the Church — and all ecumenical controversies are rooted in ecclesiology.

Much of this book's subject-matter was, originally, that of my graduate thesis in Systematic Theology, which drew much of its inspiration from the insights of Cardinal Ratzinger and Bishop

Kasper. I had no intention of developing the paper into a book until it was suggested to me that my work might prove helpful to seminarians, and indeed to anyone interested in a "hot" ecumenical topic. What I have done is expand and revise my thesis paper considerably to provide more excerpts and references to the essential texts of Tradition, to clarify certain matters, and to adapt it to a more general readership. I would take this opportunity to thank those who have supported me with their help and encouragement. Among these I would particularly mention Rev. Msgr. Paul J. Langsfeld, Professor of Systematic Theology at Mount St. Mary's Seminary in Emmitsburg, Maryland, who reviewed and approved my Master's paper; Rev. Msgr. Carroll Satterfield and Rev. Eamon McManus, Professors of Systematic Theology at Mount St. Mary's, who took great interest in my work and whose compliments gave me the confidence to undertake this work; and Rev. Peter M.J. Stravinskas, editor of the *Catholic Encyclopedia* and *The Catholic Answer* magazine, and author of several books and articles on the Faith, who read the whole book through, made valuable suggestions, and wrote its Foreword.

Thomas M. Kocik
June 29, 1996
*Solemnity of SS. Peter and Paul*

# Foreword

As Pope John XXIII convoked the Second Vatican Council, he listed several goals for that event, with the movement toward Christian unity holding a central place. Three decades after the Second Vatican Council, the Church is poised to enter upon the third millennium — but with divisions still evident. In the years immediately following the Council, a certain euphoria characterized ecumenical relations. That served as a kind of balm for the years, indeed centuries, of disunity and even rancor. And then ecumenism seemed to move off the front burner; some supposed that the present Pontiff had even removed it from the stove entirely! But in May of 1995, he surprised many observers with the promulgation of an encyclical wholly devoted to the quest for Christian unity, *Ut Unum Sint*.

While the developments of the preceding paragraph were being played out according to the plan of providence, a young boy was wending his way through a Catholic elementary school education, discerning a priestly vocation, and eventually embarking upon a program of priestly formation. He was a "child of the Council," through and through. His theological perspective was framed by the lights and shadows of the post-conciliar era in the United States, and his own specific interests drew him to an issue which many would consider somewhat "esoteric" — what we might dub the "why" and the "how" of apostolic succession, something either taken for granted or put to one side in much theological conversation today. When confronted with the need to produce a master's thesis in theology, this budding scholar decided to study in depth this precise matter. How pleased he must have been to discover as his research ended that the Holy Father concurred in his judgment that apostolic succession was a prime topic of concern for ecumenical dialogue, in fact, referred to in *Ut Unum Sint* as one of "the areas in need of fuller study before a true consensus of faith can be achieved" [n. 79].

I have had the pleasure of knowing Thomas Kocik throughout his seminary career. He is an articulate individual, who has the happy faculty of being able to take deep concepts and to make them comprehensible to folks of average intelligence, without sacrificing nuance or profundity — a rare gift. He is, above all, a loyal son of the Church who is moderate and prudent. Which is to say that he is no more Catholic than the Pope, but not one iota less so, either. In negotiating the tightrope of an ecumenically sensitive subject such as apostolic succession, our author has certainly heeded the advice of Pope John Paul II:

> In this courageous journey towards unity, the transparency and the prudence of faith require us to avoid both false irenicism and indifference to the Church's ordinances. Conversely, that same transparency and prudence urge us to reject a half-hearted commitment to unity and, even more, a prejudicial opposition or a defeatism which tends to see everything in negative terms.
>
> To uphold a vision of unity which takes account of all the demands of revealed truth does not mean to put a brake on the ecumenical movement. On the contrary, it means preventing it from settling for apparent solutions which would lead to no firm and solid results. The obligation to respect the truth is absolute. Is this not the law of the Gospel? [*Ut Unum Sint*, n. 79]

Although the reader will not find this book "a quick read" or the subject matter for cocktail parties, one will find the work most enjoyable and rewarding. Surely, clergy and seminarians, as well as theologians and those involved in pastoral work with our "separated brethren," will encounter a treasure trove of information and insight which will fulfill the Holy Father's hope for more serious research in this area, so vital to the life of the Church. How vital? One need only consider this assessment of St. Ignatius of Antioch, written within the first century:

> Let everyone revere the deacons as Jesus Christ, the bishop as the image of the Father, and the presbyters as the senate of God and the assembly of the apostles. For without them one cannot speak of the Church. [*Ad Trall.*, 3, 1]

By a happy coincidence, the author will end up correcting the galley sheets for this book even as he makes final preparations to receive the very sacrament he has so carefully and lovingly studied and presented for our reflection.

*Ad multos gloriosque annos*, Father Kocik!

Father Peter M.J. Stravinskas, Ph.D., S.T.D.
Editor, *The Catholic Answer*

# Introduction

*"For I delivered to you as of first importance what I also received..."*
— St. Paul the Apostle, to the Church at Corinth (1 Cor 15:3)

"You shall be My witnesses," our Lord said to His apostles. That witness is continuously borne by the one *apostolic Church* with which the disparate Churches claim identity.

Apostolic — what does that mean? Christians of all three major traditions — Roman Catholic, Eastern Orthodox and Protestant — can agree on this much at least: the *apostolicity* of the Church means that the faith which she teaches is the faith of the apostles, essentially unchanged through the centuries. Yet when it comes to what apostolicity means in greater detail, opinions begin to diverge.

For the Catholic, as for the Orthodox, apostolicity means something more than merely agreement with apostolic doctrine: it means also that the powers and authority which the Church's ministers receive in the sacrament of Order come by unbroken succession from the apostles themselves. This historical continuity with the Church's original witnesses and office-bearers is called the "apostolic succession."

The Churches born of the Protestant Reformation, for historical and theological reasons, do not insist on the historic succession of office as essential to the Church's structure and apostolicity. Because they lack the apostolic succession in the full Catholic sense, the Catholic Church does not recognize a valid exercise of Order and sacraments in these communities. To overcome differences here, progress must be made in what Cardinal Ratzinger calls the "key question in the Catholic-Protestant dispute": Tradition and the Apostolic Succession.[1]

What assurance does the Church have that the whole inheritance of Tradition has not undergone, in the course of the centuries, not a process of organic development, but one of accretion or corruption, such that its present form is not really the "faith which was once for all delivered to the saints" (Jude 3)? Where are the boundaries of legitimate theological pluralism to be drawn? and who is competent to draw them? The thoughtful consideration of these questions makes plain the relationship between Tradition and legitimate Church office: they are so interdependent, so mutually inherent, that one sees the wisdom in treating them as fundamentally the *one* major ecumenical question.

The apostolic succession fastens on the very heart of all ecumenical controversies: the mystery of the Church. All the mysteries which theologians examine — whether the Trinity or the Incarnation or grace or whatever — provide occasions for the Church to reflect on herself; for ecclesiology — the Church's self-understanding and self-expression — is bound up with each of them. If Christianity is defined by doctrines (though it is by no means *merely* credal), the question becomes *what* those doctrines are. And this leads immediately to the question of *who* pronounces on them. The Catholic Church's whole identity depends on the conviction that she possesses the ministry and authority of Jesus Christ. Her bishops have received their authorization in a lineal sequence from the apostles and, behind them, from Christ. As the successors of the apostles, they validly exercise the functions of the apostles: teach-

---

[1] See PCT, 239-84.

ing Jesus Christ's message and the message concerning Jesus Christ, governing the faithful according to the pattern He instituted, and sanctifying them with His divine life, especially through the sacraments.

*Apostolic Succession and the Word.* Without the apostolic succession, Christians would not have the Bible in its present and fixed form: two Testaments, four Gospels, the twenty-seven "books" of the New Testament, and so on. Why not? Because the Bible's authority and canonicity are by no means self-evident. The claim of 2 Timothy 3:16, that "all scripture is inspired by God," commands assent only if Second Timothy itself is an inspired document. Many writings claim divine inspiration, such as the Koran, the Book of Mormon, and the sacred texts of various Eastern religions. Surely, the claim alone is insufficient reason to accept them as inspired by God (and therefore inerrant). While no orthodox Christian would deny what 2 Timothy 3:16 says, it is nevertheless legitimate to ask: what body of writings did its author have in mind when he said "all scripture"? At the time of Second Timothy's composition, Christians were hardly in agreement with one another as to which of the many writings circulating among their Churches were "canonical." Moreover, some of the New Testament documents were not yet written.

The Church historian Eusebius of Caesarea, writing early in the fourth century, categorizes the manuscripts circulating in his day as, first, "those writings which according to the tradition of the Church are true, genuine, and recognized"; second, the "spurious books," neither heterodox nor divinely inspired; and third, those whose "contents are so irreconcilable with true orthodoxy that they stand revealed as the forgeries of heretics."[2] For some time, St.

---

[2] *Historia Ecclesiastica* 3.25 (with listings). Translation by G.A. Williamson, ed. Andrew Louth, rev. ed. (London: Penguin Books, 1989), 89.

Clement's Letter to the Corinthians was read in Christian churches perhaps as often as St. Paul's. The Gospel of Luke, the Acts of the Apostles, and the Apocalypse of John were eventually accepted by the whole Church, but not the Gospel of Thomas, the Acts of Paul, and the Apocalypse of Peter. The question of canonicity, then, logically implies the question of the apostolic succession. The collection of manuscripts which we know today as the Bible is a product of the living Tradition of the Church, a Tradition which requires authorized witnesses, interpreters and protagonists.

As the recognized successors of the apostles, the bishops of the early Christian Church were in a position to determine which writings to include in the canon of Scripture and which to exclude from it. The apostolic element of the Church compiled the word of God in the form of Scripture.

Perhaps a rather simplistic analogy will prove instructive. Imagine that placed before you is a large collection of photographs taken on different occasions over the past century or so. You wish to compile these photographs into a family album, but there is one problem: several of the photographs are unfamiliar, having been taken years before you saw the light of day. There is no question about the photographs which you can identify personally ("That's Aunt Margaret and Uncle Leonard at the Jersey shore"): they belong in the album. And, of course, there is always the possibility that an older relative can identify the persons and events in the old photographs. Dad can say, "That's your great-great-grandfather Samuel, after returning from the Battle of Gettysburg," because Dad received that yellowed photo from his father, who received it from his father, who received it from a battle-scarred Samuel. The family "tradition," as it were, interprets the photographs, provides them a context, and passes them down to successive generations until eventually they are compiled into a single album. Apart from this family tradition, the meaning of the photographs will remain obscure and incomplete: a man and a woman, perhaps husband and wife, at a beach somewhere; an anonymous soldier in a Civil War uniform.

It is much the same idea with the Church's Tradition and the apostolic succession. Referring to how the apostolic Tradition was passed on from one generation of believers to the next, the Second Vatican Council says:

> It was done by the apostles who handed on, by the spoken word of their preaching, by the example they gave, by the institutions they established, what they themselves had received — whether from the lips of Christ, from His way of life and His works, or whether they had learned it by the prompting of the Holy Spirit; it was done by those apostles and other men associated with the apostles who, under the inspiration of the same Holy Spirit, committed the message of salvation to writing.[3]

As one theologian succinctly put it: "The Spirit in the Church evaluates the Spirit in the testimony."[4] The Bible, then, is to be read within the Church, as interpreted by the Fathers and as understood and contextualized by the Church's Tradition of teaching and worship. Otherwise, one can expect only to "gnaw the bark of Sacred Scripture and never attain its pith,"[5] or worse, as the inspired Second Letter of Peter warns, to distort Scripture to one's own destruction (2 P 3:16). The question of Tradition — its object-content and its binding force — is so tied up with the apostolic succession that together they form the basic ecclesiological foundation underlying all ecumenical controversies.

---

[3] DV 7.

[4] Hans Urs von Balthasar, *In the Fullness of Faith: On the Centrality of the Distinctively Catholic*, trans. Graham Harrison (San Francisco: Ignatius Press, 1988), 95. (First published in German as *Katholisch* [Einsiedeln, Switzerland: Johannes Verlag, 1975].)

[5] Pope Leo XIII, Encyclical *Providentissimus Deus* (1893).

*Apostolic Succession and Sacrament.* In addition to the faithful transmission and interpretation of the apostolic word, the apostolic succession is vital to the Church for another reason. The exalted Christ communicates Himself to us not only in word but also in sacrament. "Seated at the right hand of the Father, and pouring out the Holy Spirit on His Body which is the Church," the *Catechism* teaches, "Christ now acts through the sacraments He instituted to communicate His grace."[6] By means of the apostolic succession, the Church (or rather, Christ's Spirit at work in the Church) produces the Eucharist, the Sacrament of the Lord's sacrifice which culminated on the Cross, thereby making Him really and truly present to us in a preeminent way.[7] "It is above all for this intimate communion with the Lord's life, mind and heart that 'office' exists in the Church," writes Hans Urs von Balthasar. "It is a means of communication between the Lord and those who are His, and in such a way that the very person and the existence of the one mediating it can be rendered transparent, allowing the subject of his mediation to shine through."[8] Or, as Cardinal Ratzinger elucidates:

> In order that what happened *then* may become present *now*, the words "This is My Body — this is My Blood" must be said. But the speaker of these words is the "I" of Jesus Christ. Only He can say them; they are His words. No man can dare to take to Himself the "I" and "My" of Jesus Christ — and yet the words must be said if the saving mystery is not to remain something in the distant past. So authority to pronounce them is needed, an authority which no one can assume and which no congregation, nor even many congre-

---

[6] CCC 1084.

[7] CCC 1356-81.

[8] Hans Urs von Balthasar, *Truth is Symphonic: Aspects of Christian Pluralism*, trans. Graham Harrison (San Francisco: Ignatius Press, 1987), 101. (German: *Die Wahrheit ist symphonisch. Aspekte des christlichen Pluralismus* [Einsiedeln, Switzerland: Johannes Verlag, 1972].)

gations together, can confer. Only Jesus Christ Himself, in the "sacramental" form He has committed to the whole Church, can give this authority. The word must be located, as it were, in sacrament; it must be part of the "sacrament" of the Church, partaking of an authority which she does not create, but only transmits. This is what is meant by "ordination" and "priesthood."[9]

***Purpose of the Study.*** The purpose of this book is to study the apostolic succession (which always involves the broader categories of Tradition and ecclesiology) as the central issue in ecumenism. Such an endeavor requires an examination of the apostolic succession as it was understood and lived through the Christian ages. The Church's living Tradition and the apostolic succession are not really juxtaposed; they are tightly interwoven. That is why, at several points throughout this study, there is the temptation to spend too much time at certain "trees" in the forest of ecumenical topics, all of which have their roots in the problem of Tradition. But these trees are more properly deserving of whole studies in themselves, and so the reader is referred, by way of footnotes, to a sampling of the many relevant works already in print.

***Outline.*** Our examination of the apostolic succession begins with the concept of apostleship as found in both the Old and New Testaments (*Chapter One*). Just who was an "apostle"? How did one become an apostle?

Next, we are concerned with how the early Church understood her apostolicity. Who were (and are) the successors of the apostles? By what process does one enter into the apostolic succession? Here the writings of the early Church Fathers (*Chapter Two*), together with the witness of the Church's liturgy (*Chapter Three*), are especially helpful.

---

[9] Joseph Cardinal Ratzinger, *Feast of Faith: Approaches to a Theology of the Liturgy*, trans. Graham Harrison (San Francisco: Ignatius Press, 1986), 94. (First published in German as *Das Fest des Glaubens* [Einsiedeln, Switzerland: Johannes Verlag, 1981].)

The millennium from St. Augustine to the late Middle Ages saw no real evolution of the concept of apostolic succession *per se*. However, the sacrament of Order was subject to considerable theological development beginning with the age of Christian Scholasticism in the early-twelfth century. We are concerned with this period (*Chapter Four*) only so far as the medieval theology about Order affects on the apostolic succession.

With the Protestant Reformation in the sixteenth century, not only this particular doctrine or that one, but the whole Church, became the object of theological reflection. The bishops of the Catholic Church, assembled at the Council of Trent, and later at the First and Second Vatican Councils, gave doctrinal definition to the apostolic succession (*Chapter Five*), which hitherto had been not so much an object of theological synthesis as the very form of Tradition.

Christianity is a religion of fixed dogma and of open theological questions also. Therefore, in presenting the contemporary discussion of the subject-matter (*Chapter Six*), the effort has been made to operate under what Cardinal Ratzinger calls a "hermeneutic of union": steering the middle course between a "confessional chauvinism" which accentuates what divides the Churches, and an irenicism which sacrifices truth for a pseudo-unity that can only fail.[10] Neither extreme can do justice to the quest for the unity which our Lord demands of His followers.

After reviewing some significant ecumenical dialogues (*Chapter Seven*), we consider some proposals for reconciling the separated Churches to visible unity, noting the problems associated with each proposal, and concluding with a recommendation for safeguarding the integrity of the apostolic succession in the future (*Chapter Eight*).

---

[10] PCT, 202-03.

***Presupposition.*** By way of concluding these preliminary remarks, honesty dictates that all cards be placed on the ecumenical table, as it were. Indeed it is quite unfashionable nowadays to speak of the "one true Church." The term, so some have argued, is archaic and is best left behind with the polemics of the Counter-Reformation period. It betokens narrow-mindedness and hostility (or at least indifference) to the ecclesiology of Vatican II and to the cause of Christian unity. The modern attitude shuns such rhetoric.

This book has been written with the conviction that this attitude, which is widely mistaken for Christian charity, is not real charity. It is a pretense only, an excuse for persistence in error, and consequently a detriment to that true unity which is unity-in-truth. Christians need to know where to look in order to sift the theological wheat from the chaff. We can speak of a "true Church," in the sense that there exists a single visible communion which has preserved the totality and integrity of the apostolic faith, of the sacraments and of the pastoral office instituted by Christ.

That society of Christians which follows and proclaims the Gospel, whole and unadulterated, is the Church of Jesus Christ. She is *one*: for there is only one Body of Christ. She is *holy*: for she was founded by the Holy One, and her presence in the world sanctifies it and produces countless saints despite the sins and imperfections of her members. She is *catholic*: for, unlike the sects which have broken away from her, she is an "open" society; and, realizing that "there is no salvation save in balance,"[11] she proclaims the whole divine revelation and not just pet components of it. And she is *apostolic*: for the Savior established her "upon the foundation of the apostles and prophets" (Eph 2:20), and her doctrines are theirs.

---

[11] St. Gregory Nazianzen, *Second Discourse* 34: PG 35, 441b-c.

In addition to these four classic marks, the Church is also called *orthodox*: for, unlike heretical congregations, she is guided by the Spirit of Truth to teach the truth about God and creation. She is also *evangelical*: for she says nothing on her own account, but announces only the Good News of her Bridegroom. And she is *reformed* — in fact, *semper reformanda*: for she continually renews her institutions, customs and practices, not in condescension to modern times, but in order "to impart an ever-increasing vigor to the Christian life."[12]

The apostolic succession makes it possible for the faith of Christ and the Church of the New Testament to exist even unto the consummation of the world. The Catholic Church, in all humility, believes herself to be this Church, the Church of the apostolic Tradition, the "one, holy, catholic and apostolic Church" of which the Niceno-Constantinopolitan Creed speaks. Therefore, in speaking of unity, what is meant is not unity in the strict sense of the word, but rather "union" or "reunion." The unity of the Church has not been lost, because she is "the Body of Christ, the fullness of Him" (Eph 1:23), and as such cannot be divided. Of course, divisions among Christians have broken the unity of faith and the integrity of Order. But the visible unity of the Church has not been lost, so as now to be a problem of search and discovery.[13] Catholicism does not drive a wedge between the "invisible" and the "visible" Church. The problem of unity is, therefore, the problem of the return to the *fullness* of apostolic faith and Order, which is found in the visible communion of the apostolic Catholic Church.[14]

---

[12] Vatican II, "Constitution on the Sacred Liturgy," *Sacrosanctum Concilium*, no. 1.

[13] Congregation for the Doctrine of the Faith, "Declaration in Defense of the Catholic Doctrine of the Church against Certain Errors of the Present Day," *Mysterium Ecclesiae* (June 24, 1973). Pope John Paul II reaffirms this in UUS 14.

[14] Cf. UUS 86.

To occupy the papacy, or even a bishopric, in the early centuries of the Church was the same as consenting to violent and bloody death, invariably lying in wait for each successor of the Apostles of Jesus Christ. What an enticement to office!... On such pure and blazing Faith, on such supreme and invincible courage was the early Church foundationed. Such is our heritage!

— *Sister Catherine Goddard Clarke, M.I.C.M.*

We, therefore, profess to conserve and guard the rules bequeathed to the Holy Catholic and Apostolic Church by the Holy and most illustrious Apostles, by the orthodox Councils, both general and local, and by every one of those divine interpreters, the Fathers and Doctors of the Church.

— *Fourth Council of Constantinople*

Chapter One

# Apostleship in the New Testament

## 1.1. The meaning of "apostle"

It makes good sense to begin our examination of the apostolic succession with the question: what and who is an apostle? Etymologically speaking, an apostle is "one who is sent" (Greek *apostolos*; Hebrew *saliah*). The author of the Letter to the Hebrews calls Jesus Christ the Apostle of God (3:1).

Jesus formed a special group of twelve disciples and gave them a share in His mission of reconciling the world to God (2 Cor 5:18-19). "And He appointed twelve, to be with Him, and to be sent out [*apostellē*] to preach" (Mk 3:14; cf. Mt 10:1). St. John's Gospel links the apostles' mission from Christ with Christ's mission from the Father: "As the Father has sent [*apestalken*] Me, even so I send [*pempō*] you" (20:21). Therefore, our Savior told them, "He who receives you receives Me, and he who receives Me receives Him Who sent [*aposteilanta*] Me" (Mt 10:40; cf. Lk 10:16; Jn 13:20). It would go better with the Sodomites and Gomorrheans than with the city that would not give ear to the apostles (Lk 10:10-16; Mt 10:15).

Yet others, too, were sent out by Jesus: "After this the Lord appointed seventy others, and sent [*apesteilen*] them on ahead of Him, two by two..." (Lk 10:1). Thus it would be a mistake to identify "the apostles" exclusively with the Twelve who were called out from the wider circle of Jesus' disciples.

St. Paul refers to the special place of the Twelve in the Church in connection with the witnesses to the Resurrection in 1 Corinthians 15:3-5:

> For I delivered to you as of first importance what I also received, that Christ died for our sins in accordance with the scriptures, that He was buried, that He was raised on the third day in accordance with the scriptures, and that He appeared to Cephas, then to the Twelve.

Besides the Twelve associated with the mother Church at Jerusalem, Paul too had the privilege of seeing the risen Lord and was charged by Him to proclaim the paschal message. As he tells the Galatian Christians (Gal 1:15-17):

> But when He Who had set me apart before I was born, and had called me through His grace, was pleased to reveal His Son to me, in order that I might preach Him among the Gentiles, I did not confer with flesh and blood, nor did I go up to Jerusalem to those who were apostles before me, but I went away into Arabia; and again I returned to Damascus.

Thus Paul frequently and emphatically refers to himself as an apostle, especially in the introductions to his letters. He admits the apostleship of the Twelve, and of Peter (Cephas) specifically (Gal 1:18; 2:8). In addition to Peter and the rest of the Twelve, Paul also acknowledges the otherwise unknown Andronicus and Junias (Rm 16:7) as apostles; then less clearly Barnabas (1 Cor 9:6; Gal 2:9), who was his companion on the first missionary journey (Ac 12 - 14); James the Lord's "brother" or kinsman (Gal 1:19; 1 Cor 15:7); John (Gal 2:9); and Silas, who replaced Barnabas (Ac 15). Paul contrasts with them the "false apostles" who have received no authorization from Christ (2 Cor 11:13). These were presumably Palestinian opponents of Paul who appealed to the authority of the "super apostles" (cf. 2 Cor 11:5; 12:11). The true apostles' credentials consist of "signs and wonders and mighty works" (2 Cor 12:12), together with a willingness to suffer for the sake of Christ (2 Cor 4:10; 7:5). Set apart (Gal 7:15), called (Rm 1:1; 1 Cor 1:1; Gal 1:15) and sent by God (1 Cor 1:17; Gal 2:8), the apostle must be totally dedicated to the Gospel of Christ. He is the servant of all, who considers it normal to be maligned and misunderstood (1 Cor 4:9-10).

The Pauline apostle was "a missionary figure, founding communities, but then moving on and maintaining contact with his communities through letters, emissaries, and occasional visits."[1] In some of the local Churches founded by Paul and his companions, as we shall see, auxiliaries to the apostles were charged with taking up where the apostles left off, being responsible for the continued care of those Churches. These apostolic auxiliaries understood their role as subordinate to that of the apostles. As one Church historian writes:

> Yet the role of these co-workers was different from that of the Twelve. Without a direct mandate from the risen Lord, they remained subject to a higher apostolic authority. Nevertheless, these co-workers shared in the apostolic ministry of preaching and pastoring.[2]

The evangelist St. Luke, Paul's longtime companion and the author of the bipartite "Luke-Acts," in the main restricts apostleship to the Twelve only — an exception being his reference to Paul and

---

[1] Raymond E. Brown, S.S., *Priest and Bishop: Biblical Reflections* (New York: Paulist Press, 1970), 35.

[2] J. Michael Miller, C.S.B., *The Shepherd and the Rock: Origins, Development, and Mission of the Papacy* (Huntington, IN: Our Sunday Visitor, Inc., 1995), 56.

Barnabas as apostles (Ac 14:4, 14). To his account of the calling of the Twelve, Luke adds the detail that Jesus named them "apostles" (Lk 6:13). This word occurs only once in each of the other three Gospels, but Luke repeatedly refers to the inner-circle of disciples as the "twelve apostles." The Acts of the Apostles relates that the Twelve stayed first of all in Jerusalem (8:1), and somewhat reluctantly undertook the mission to the Gentiles (10:1-11; 18). It is said only of Peter and John that they left Jerusalem (8:14-25). Scripture scholar Fr. Raymond Brown reckons that the Twelve were not so much missionaries to the Gentiles as decision-makers in matters affecting the whole Church, such as in the appointment of the seven assistants (Ac 6:1-6) and in the resolution of the Gentile controversy (Ac 15:1-12).[3]

Of what does the apostolic mission consist? The mission of the apostles is none other than the mission of Christ. The synoptic Gospels provide the theological basis for the threefold office (*munus triplex*) ascribed in Tradition to Christ: Priest, Prophet and King.[4]

First, Jesus gave the Twelve a participation in His priestly office, entrusting to them the worship or *cultus* of the New Covenant. At the Last Supper, they were commanded to celebrate the Eucharist for His *anamnêsis* (Lk 22:19) — something much stronger in biblical Greek than our word "remembrance" — thereby bringing Him, and the power of His saving sacrifice, into our present time. On another occasion, they received also the command to baptize (Mt 28:19; Mk 16:16; Jn 3:22; 4:2). They were to exer-

---

[3] Brown, *Priest and Bishop*, 51-58.

[4] CCC 436. Here we shall closely follow the fine treatment of this theme in Aidan Nichols, O.P., *Holy Order: The Apostolic Ministry from the New Testament to the Second Vatican Council*. Oscott Series, gen. eds. Maurice Couve de Murville (Abp. of Birmingham), Frs. David McLoughlin and David Evans, no. 5 (Dublin: Veritas, 1990), 6-12.

cise the priestly task of sanctification, moreover, by healing the sick and exorcising demons (Mt 10:1, 8; Mk 6:13).

Secondly, the Twelve were given a unique teaching role corresponding to Christ as God's Prophet *par excellence.* Jesus sent them out to preach His doctrine (Mt 28:20; Mk 16:15; Lk 24:47). For Jews of old, there was a mystical identification of an emissary with the sender. Anyone who receives the Twelve receives the Master (Mt 10:40; cf. Lk 10:16; Jn 13:20).

Thirdly, corresponding to Christ's kingly or pastoral role, the Twelve were also given authority to govern the New Covenant community which is the Church (Mt 19:28; Lk 22:28-30). Their genuine governing authority is ordered to the promotion of that unity which reflects the unbreakable unity of Father and Son.

St. John's Gospel also portrays the ministry of the Twelve as a share in the priestly, prophetic and pastoral office of Christ. Although the Fourth Gospel provides no account of the institution of the Eucharist, the English Dominican scholar Aidan Nichols claims that

> the evangelist takes it for granted that his readers know of that great happening at the Last Supper. It is in this presumed context that he portrays Jesus as praying that the Twelve may be consecrated as He is consecrated — that is, set apart from the world for the service of the Father, through which others will find spiritual life, truth, and unity.[5]

The reference to Jesus' "High Priestly Prayer" (Jn 17) is significant because of its indebtedness to the four Songs of the Suffering Servant in the Book of Isaiah (42:1-4; 49:1-6; 50:4-9; 52:13 - 53:12).[6]

---

[5] Nichols, 8-9.

[6] The connection to the Book of Isaiah has been argued persuasively by the French exegete André Feuillet, *The Priesthood of Christ and His Ministers*, trans. Matthew J. O'Connell (Garden City, NY: Doubleday & Co., 1975). Cited in Nichols, 9.

The Servant is reminiscent of the prophet Jeremiah and of Judah's last independent king, Jehoiachim. Primarily, though, he is a priestly figure, offering a sacrifice of expiation. Unlike the Levitical priests, who offer the blood of animals, the Servant voluntarily offers his own life in atonement for the sins of his people, thereby saving them from just punishment at the hands of God. The Christological connotation is obvious: Jesus consecrates Himself as an expiatory sacrifice, so that from His consecration the disciples may receive the necessary sanctification and dedication. Thus the Suffering Servant incorporates the threefold *munus* of prophet, king and (especially) priest.

In the High Priestly Prayer of chapter 17, the Servant is realized ideally in the Son of God. Christ foretells a divine mission for the disciples, a mission that will be given on Easter night after His sacrifice has been completed.[7]

> The priestly office of the Twelve is a fruit of Christ's sacrifice on the Cross — a consideration which points to its special relationship with the Eucharist as understood by the later Church.[8]

On the evening of the Resurrection, Christ bestowed the Holy Spirit on the apostles for the forgiveness of sins (20:19-23). He came into the world to reconcile repentant sinners with God; now He transferred to the apostles this great mission.

The whole of the Fourth Gospel portrays Jesus as the pre-existent Word (*Logos*) Who reveals the Father; the apostles are now to be teachers and prophets, making known the communion of the Father and the Son — and the communion of believers with the Father and the Son — through the Spirit-inspired word of their

---

[7] Raymond E. Brown, S.S., *The Gospel and Epistles of John: A Concise Commentary* (Collegeville, MN: The Liturgical Press, 1988), 86.

[8] Nichols, 10.

preaching (17:20). After receiving from Peter a triple profession of love to make up for his triple denial, Jesus committed to him, as leader of the Twelve, the pastoral charge of the whole Church (21:15-17). In communion with Peter, the apostles are to render the Church a unity.

## 1.2. Successors of the apostles

If we are going to speak of successors of the apostles, we should first realize that there are two constitutive elements of an apostle's call which cannot be passed on: witnessing the risen Christ and receiving immediately from Him the commission to evangelize. Thus apostleship in the sense of the original ministry of the first eyewitnesses and emissaries came to an end with the death of the last apostle.

But acknowledging the uniqueness of the apostles' identity does not exclude the continuance of their charge. The Pastoral Letters (the First and Second Letters to Timothy, and the Letter to Titus) manifest the original apostles' intention to preserve their mission through the appointment of successors. In these letters we find signs of later Catholic doctrine and practice. As Fr. J. Michael Miller writes:

> Timothy and Titus, disciples and co-workers of Paul during his lifetime, both carried on his work after his death, having authority to "appoint elders in every town" (Tt 1:5). A principal obligation of Timothy and Titus was to guarantee the Church's continuity and expansion by choosing suitable men to exercise pastoral ministry in local communities (cf. 1 Tm 3:1-13, 5:22; Tt 1:5-9). The first apostles and disciples associated them with the apostolic ministry by the laying-on of hands (cf. 1 Tm 4:14; 2 Tm 1:6). Those associated with Paul's ministry either directly or through his

co-workers were the "elders" and/or "bishops" who were recognized as Paul's successors in teaching and leadership. Regardless of the terminology used, only those who were duly appointed and carried out the fullness of apostolic ministry are true successors to the apostolic mission.[9]

The titles "bishop" (Greek *episkopos*, "supervisor") and "elder" (Greek *presbuteros*) were not sharply differentiated in the first-century Church. This terminological ambiguity becomes evident when we compare different Pauline letters. As early as his First Letter to the Thessalonians (ca. 51), Paul exhorts that community to respect those who labor among them and preside over (*proistamenous*) them in the Lord (5:12). These same words are used of the *presbuteros* in the First Letter to Timothy (5:17). To point out the probable connection between the "presidents in the Lord" at Thessalonica and the Apostle Paul's authority, we turn to its sister Church at Corinth, where Paul never mentions the presence of *episkopoi*. On the basis of this silence, some would consider the orderly succession of bishops (as they would later be called) a post-apostolic development.[10] Were the Corinthians without pastoral supervisors, *episkopoi*, functioning as duly-authorized local versions of Paul's own apostleship?

Brown speculates that perhaps Paul had stayed at Corinth for a length of time (a year and a half), so that the Church there was well established. In other places, however, Paul had to move on hastily, appointing men to lead those communities in his absence. If this hypothesis is correct, then Corinth may have been an exception to the rule among the Pauline Churches.[11]

Nichols offers an alternative explanation. Stephanas, Fortu-

---

[9] Miller, 57.

[10] On this Nichols cites Edward Schillebeeckx, *Ministry, A Case for Change* (London, 1981) and *The Church with a Human Face: A New and Expanded Theology of Ministry* (London, 1985).

[11] Brown, *Priest and Bishop*, 70-71.

natus and Achaicus (1 Cor 16:15-17) are indeed the *episkopoi* at Corinth, in view of what Paul says in his Letter to the Philippians. This letter is addressed to "all the saints in Christ Jesus who are at Philippi, with the *episkopoi* and *diakonoi*" (1:1).

> Assuming that the apostolic "structures" given by Paul to the Churches of Philippi and Corinth are cognate — both were the fruit of his second and third missionary journeys — these terms of address can illuminate the named leaders and their anonymous helpers at Corinth. Stephanas, together with his fellow-workers of comparable standing, appear to be overseers, presbyters with *episkopé*, and in this sense *episkopoi*, whilst those members of Stephanas' household co-opted as instruments of his ministry would correspond, then, to the Philippian "deacons."[12]

Whereas Paul is silent about the *episkopoi* at Corinth, he makes no mention of *presbuteroi* at Philippi.

Here it is worth mentioning that the offices of *episkopos* and *presbuteros* have pre-Christian antecedents. The *episkopos* was an overseer in the secular sense, as used in the Septuagint (Nb 31:14; Ne 11:9-22; 1 M 1:51), whose responsibility was to provide for the general good order of society. In the Jewish sect at Qumran, described in the Dead Sea Scrolls (1 QS 6.12-20), this task was performed by the *mebaqqer* ("overseer" — the literal sense of the Greek term also), or *paqid*. In the Damascus Document, the *mebaqqer* is likened to a shepherd (CD 13.9-10); the same image of shepherding is used of Christian *episkopoi* in Acts 20:28 and 1 Peter 5:2-4.

The *presbuteros*, on the other hand, exercised authority in the synagogue because of the wisdom usually associated with his age (hence the English rendering of the word as "elder"). While his was a position *honoris causa*, its importance should not be underesti-

---

[12] Nichols, 27.

mated. In Jerusalem the elders ranked, after the high-priests and scribes, third in what became the Supreme Council (*Sanhedrin*). The *presbuteroi* had a long history in Judaism, going back to the monumental events of the Passover and the Sinai Covenant (Ex 12:21; 19:7).

The influence of these antecedents on the primitive Church is the subject of debate among scholars. Fr. Hans Küng, for example, argues that the *episkopoi* functioned at first in Gentile Christianity, and only sometime later was their office adopted in Jewish Christianity. Underlying this thesis is the premise that *episkopos* and *presbuteros* were distinct offices even in the New Testament period: the former borrowed from Gentile secular and religious organization, whereas the latter borrowed from Judaism.[13]

Brown disagrees, on the grounds that this thesis ignores the evidence of the Dead Sea Scrolls. It is an oversimplification to hold that the Church derived her episcopate (strictly) from the pagan and secular sphere, and her presbyterate from Judaism. At Qumran there were, besides presbyters, *episkopoi* under the name of *mebaqqer*. Thus Brown theorizes:

> From the synagogue Christians borrowed a pattern of groups of presbyters for each Church, while the pastoral-supervisor (*episkopos*) role given to all or many of these presbyters came from the organizational model of close-knit Jewish sectarian groups such as the Dead Sea Essenes.[14]

The tendency in modern investigation of early Church organization is to regard the *episkopoi* as elders (*presbuteroi*) possessed of *episkopē*, that is, powers of governance. Because of their govern-

---

[13] Hans Küng, *The Church*, trans. Ray and Rosaleen Ockenden (New York: Sheed & Ward, 1967), 400.

[14] Raymond E. Brown, S.S., *The Churches the Apostles Left Behind* (New York: Paulist Press, 1984), 33; cf. *idem, Priest and Bishop*, 68-69.

ing role, these Church elders or presbyters were called *episkopoi*, "overseers" or "guardians." The New Testament in general, as well as non-biblical sources, suggest the equivalency of *episkopos* and *presbuteros*.[15] As Paul instructs the Ephesian presbyters in Acts 20:28:

> Take heed to yourselves and to all the flock, in which the Holy Spirit has made you guardians [*episkopoi*], to feed the Church of the Lord which He obtained with His own blood.

Thus, what were two distinct functions in first-century Judaism merged together in the early Church. Some time later, there would be a realignment of these roles. As Nichols explains:

> Within the New Testament corpus, the overall contrast is that between the universal apostolic ministry — the Twelve, the wider apostleship, the auxiliary apostles and apostolic delegates — and the local ministry of presbyters, presbyters with *episkopê* or overseers and deacons. Since this is the dominant contrast, it is predictable that the authors of the material will tend to telescope the local ministries, and notably those of presbyter and overseer. Only later, when the apostles have disappeared from the scene will the distinction between eldership and *episkopê* be expressed as a difference in order.[16]

The presbyter-supervisors were charged with safeguarding the apostolic Tradition against error and with governing the Churches the apostles founded and left behind. They were the Church's earliest bishops, who, while not apostles themselves, understood that they had succeeded to the apostolic ministry of teaching, sanctifying and governing the faithful.

---

[15] The second-century Roman document of Hermas, *The Shepherd*, refers to presbyters specifically as *proistamenôn tês ekklêsias*, "leaders of the Church" ("Visions" 2.4.3).

[16] Nichols, 29-30.

## 1.3. Ordination

The process whereby ministers of religion are appointed is called "ordination." How were the apostles and their successors ordained? One would search the New Testament in vain for an account of Jesus ordaining the Twelve (or Paul) by the ritual gesture familiar to us today: that is, by prayer and the laying-on of hands. Should we conclude, then, that the sacrament of Order has no scriptural basis and perhaps (worse yet) no derivation from Jesus Himself, in which case it is not truly a sacrament?

Catholic theology permits us to conceive the notion of sacramentality in broader terms. To claim that Jesus Christ "instituted" a sacrament does not necessarily mean that He established the external rite. Rather, it means that something in His life justifies the Church's use of a particular ritual action.[17] Jesus empowered the apostles to share in the fullness of His unique Priesthood, to speak in His name and to act in His person, as we saw earlier with the threefold *munus*. Understanding ordination in this wider sense, one can scarcely take issue with the Church's Tradition of recognizing the ordination of the Twelve in successive stages.[18]

How did the Twelve and the other apostles ordain their suc-

---

[17] CCC 1115: "The mysteries of Christ's life are the foundations of what He would henceforth dispense in the sacraments, through the ministers of His Church, for 'what was visible in our Savior has passed over into His mysteries' [St. Leo the Great, *Sermo* 74.2; PL 54, 398]."

When Christ is seen as the primordial Sacrament, and the Church as a "root" sacrament from which spring various sacramental acts, it is not necessary to search for a word of the historical Jesus to secure the institution of the seven sacraments. Commenting on the Scholastic tradition in Latin Catholicism, Herbert Vorgrimler notes that institution "could also be seen in the fact that God gave the sacraments their effective power, something that is equally impossible to fix at a particular moment in time, and that in some instances this is ascribed to the work of the exalted Christ through the Spirit" — *Sacramental Theology*, trans. Linda M. Maloney (Collegeville, MN: The Liturgical Press, 1992), 74. Although the Councils of Florence and Trent taught that Jesus instituted the seven sacraments, no one definition of the word *institutio* has ever been canonized. Also see A. Schmied, "Was ist ein Sakrament?" *Theologie der Gegenwart* 20 (1977): 151-52.

cessors? When someone was needed to replace the betrayer Judas Iscariot, the eleven members of the inner-circle drew lots to decide between Joseph Barsabbas and Matthias (Ac 1:15-26). To modern-day Christians, the election by lottery to such an important position will, no doubt, appear haphazard or even superstitious. But we, unlike the Eleven, are far removed from ancient Judaism, which saw in the casting of lots the opportunity for God's will to be disclosed without human manipulation (cf. 1 S 14:41-42). Because Luke stresses the laying-on of hands for the conferral of the apostolate (Ac 6:1-6; 13:3), it is not difficult to conjecture that Matthias was received into the apostolic college by this gesture. But this is not known for certain.

The Pastoral Letters indicate the laying-on of hands as the only method of ordination. Two passages from the Letters to Timothy are important and should be seen as complementing each other. The first is 1 Timothy 4:14:

> Do not neglect the gift you have, which was given you by prophetic utterance when the elders [*presbuteroi*] laid their hands on you.

The other is 2 Timothy 1:6:

> Hence I remind you to rekindle the gift of God that is within you through the laying-on of my hands.

It is unclear from these two passages who ordained Timothy: Paul? the presbyters? the prophets? Perhaps a reconstruction might be ventured: Timothy was called through prophecy, ordained by Paul

---

[18] On Lk 22:19 as "ordination" in terms of conferral by Christ of the priestly office, particularly for the celebration of the Eucharist, see Council of Trent, Sess. XXII, *Canones de Ss. Missæ sacrificio*, can. 2 (DS 1752); cf. Sess. XXIII, *Doctrina de sacramento ordinis*, cap. 1 (DS 1764); also CCC 611, 1341. On Jn 20:22 as "ordination" understood as receiving from Christ the threefold office, see CCC 730, 1120 and 1461.

(2 Tm 1:6: *dia tês epitheseôs tôn cheirôn mou*), and "confirmed" in his office by the local presbyterate (1 Tm 4:14: *meta epitheseôs tôn cheirôn*).[19] At the same time, Timothy is warned that he should not "be hasty in the laying-on of hands" (1 Tm 5:22), for this is a solemn gesture with serious effects.

How did the early Church come to use this rite for the ordination of her ministers? In Judaism, the imposition of hands (Hebrew *semikhah*) was a gesture used in sacrificial offerings and in the deputation of officials for religious and public life, such as judges, elders and rabbis. Jews trace this ceremony back to the time of Moses. In the Book of Numbers, God instructs Moses to appoint seventy elders to share in the governing of the people, and God bestowed on them some of the spirit that was in Moses (Nb 11:16-25). Later, Joshua is selected to rule over the Israelites and "he [Moses] laid his hands upon him [Joshua], and commissioned him as the Lord directed through Moses" (Nb 27:23). A parallel passage in Deuteronomy reads: "And Joshua the son of Nun was full of the spirit of wisdom, for Moses had laid his hands upon him" (Dt 34:9). This became the standard procedure for commissioning the leaders of God's people. A rabbi would ordain his own pupils. As time progressed, degrees of leadership were acknowledged. For the highest level of authority, a formula was employed which gave the candidate authority in both judicial and religious affairs: *"Yoreh yoreh yaddin yaddin"* ("He may surely decide and he may surely judge").[20]

In an effort to stamp out the influence and authority of the Sanhedrin, the Emperor Hadrian (ca. 135) made the imposition of hands a criminal act punishable by death. Although done clan-

---

[19] The *meta* of 1 Tm 4:14 probably signifies accompaniment rather than instrumental causality — just as presbyters at modern-day ordinations do not ordain, but they do impose hands after ordination as a gesture of collegiality.

[20] *New Standard Jewish Encyclopedia*, 1970 ed., s.v. "Ordination."

destinely, the rite was observed at least until the time of Patriarch Hillel II in the latter part of the fourth century. Then, because of its adoption by Christians, ordination by the laying-on of hands fell into disfavor among Jews, whereafter the gesture was supplanted by the granting of a rabbinical degree or diploma.[21]

## Summary

An apostle, by definition, is one who is sent. Luke normally applies the title "apostle" to the Twelve, though he recognizes Paul and Barnabas as apostles. For the Apostle Paul, as for Luke, the immediate calling by the Lord Jesus is the essential constituent of the apostolate. In the Pauline Letters we find a comprehensive theology of apostleship. The apostle is an emissary of Christ, as Christ is the Emissary of the Father. The apostolic vocation is substantiated by miracles and wonders. Day by day, the apostle is called to suffer for the cause of the Gospel.

Even before the existence of a structured community, Christ prepared the organ responsible for orthodox faith (and His sacramental presence is part of this faith), the episcopal (= supervising) office, through the calling of the Twelve and the attribution of full powers to them (Mk 3:14-15). These powers were Christological: the authorization to proclaim Christ's heavenly doctrine in His name and to combat the spirit of the Antichrist with His power, in the Holy Spirit.

This means that Jesus granted a participation in His messianic function, that of representing God and His saving work to His people. Hence the apostolic office will always be primarily an office of representing God from now on concretely in Christ. This

---

[21] *Universal Jewish Encyclopedia*, 1948 ed., s.v. "Ordination."

office was held by the *episkopoi*, the presbyter-bishops, the primary caretakers and leaders of the Churches founded by the apostles. It is in this sense that we understand them as successors of the apostles. The laying-on of hands, a ceremonial action going back to Moses, was the conventional means of entrance into the apostolic ministry — "ordination" — in the primitive Church. It is time now to examine the notions of apostolicity and the apostolic succession as found in the copious testimony of the early Christian apologists.

## Chapter Two

# Apostolicity in the Early Christian Literature

The examples and teaching of the early Church Fathers provide us with a picture of Christian theology and life in the post-apostolic period. The Fathers of the Church are witnesses and protagonists of the apostolic Tradition, having transmitted what they received from the apostles and their immediate successors. Because they are closer to the sources in their purity, "the Church has always referred to the Fathers as a guarantee of truth."[1] Patristic thought was always Christ-centered. The essence of the apostolic succession is Christ's promise to remain with His Church (Mt 28:20: "I am with you always"), so that "he who hears you hears Me..." (Lk 10:16; cf. Mt 10:40; Jn 13:20).[2]

We will be looking at the period from the end of the first century, when (as St. Irenaeus put it) the echo of the apostles' preaching was still audible,[3] to the middle of the third century, when the Church was involved in her struggles with Gnosticism and other

---

[1] Congregation for Catholic Education, *Instruction on the Study of the Fathers of the Church in the Formation of Priests* (Nov. 10, 1989), 2.1(e); *Origins* 19 (1990): 549-61, quote at 554.

[2] Antonio Javierre, S.D.B., "La thème de la succession des apôtres dans la litterature chrétienne primitive," in *L'Épiscopat et l'Église Universelle* (Paris: Editions du Cerf, 1962), 197: "Le Christ s'est lui-même promis à ses disciples en leur disant: 'Qui vous accueille, m'accueille.' Et le Christ a aussi engagé sa présence, en disant, 'Je suis avec vous...' La liaison de ces deux promesses, dans le sentiment des Pères, conduit à la succession."

[3] *Adversus Hæreses* 3.3.3; PG 7, 849.

heretical movements. The Fathers of the early Church consistently stressed the historical continuity with the apostles and their doctrine as the touchstone of orthodoxy. Their understanding of the apostolic succession is our primary interest at this time.

## 2.1. St. Clement of Rome

The end of the first century saw the Church at Corinth once again racked by fierce dissensions. Some of the Corinthian presbyters were ousted from office. This crisis prompted the fraternal but authoritative intervention of one of the earliest among St. Peter's successors. The Letter of the Roman Church to the Corinthians (ca. 96) is considered to be the most important first-century Christian document outside the New Testament, and was widely read in Christian antiquity. Although not explicitly indicating the author's identity, it is commonly attributed to the martyr Clement (died 97), the presiding presbyter or bishop of Rome (whom Eusebius identifies[4] with the Clement mentioned in Philippians 4:3).

Insisting that the procedure for the orderly succession of bishops was established by the apostles themselves, Pope Clement ordered the reinstatement of these deposed ministers. "Here for the first time," writes the Jesuit patrologist Johannes Quasten, "we find a clear and explicit declaration of the doctrine of apostolic succession."[5] As Clement tells the Corinthians:

> The apostles preached to us the Gospel received from Jesus Christ, and Jesus Christ was God's Ambassador. Christ, in other words, comes with a message from God and the apostles with a message from Christ. Both of these orderly

---

[4] *Hist. eccl.* 3.4.

[5] Johannes Quasten, S.J., *Patrology*, vol. 1, *The Beginnings of Patristic Literature* (Utrecht: Spectrum, 1950; reprint, Westminster, Md.: Christian Classics, Inc., 1992), 45.

arrangements, therefore, originate from the will of God. And so, after receiving their instructions and being fully assured through the Resurrection of our Lord Jesus Christ, as well as confirmed in faith by the word of God, they went forth, equipped with the fullness of the Holy Spirit, to preach the good news that the Kingdom of God was close at hand. From land to land, accordingly, and from city to city they preached, and from their earliest converts appointed men whom they had tested by the Spirit to act as bishops and deacons for the future believers. And this was no innovation, for a long time before the Scripture had spoken about bishops and deacons; for somewhere it says: "I will establish their overseers in observance of the law and their ministers in fidelity."[6]

Drawing out the relevance of these words for the Corinthian Church, Clement goes on to say that the Corinthian dissenters had no right to depose their overseers because the apostolic ministry is bestowed by the Lord Himself.

Our apostles, too, were given to understand by our Lord Jesus Christ that the office of the bishop would give rise to intrigues. For this reason, equipped as they were with perfect foreknowledge, they appointed the men mentioned before, and afterwards laid down a rule once for all to this effect: when these men die, other approved men shall succeed to their sacred ministry. Consequently, we deem it an injustice to eject from the sacred ministry the persons who were appointed either by them, or later, with the consent of the whole Church, by other men in high repute.[7]

The Corinthian hierarchy are referred to as bishops (*episkopoi*) and deacons (*diakonoi*). Elsewhere, they are called presbyters (*presbuteroi*) collectively. The terminological equivalency of *episkopoi* and *presbuteroi* in the first century was noted earlier. The letter at-

---

[6] *1 Clement* 42.1-4; Quasten, 1:45-46.

[7] *Ibid.* 44.1-3; Quasten, 1:46.

tributed to Clement suggests that the monarchical episcopate or "monepiscopacy" — a single bishop presiding over a college of presbyters and deacons — had not yet emerged as the standard organization of the universal Church.


## 2.2. St. Ignatius of Antioch

With Ignatius (ca. 35 - ca. 110), third bishop of Antioch (counting the Apostle Peter), we find for the first time a definite threefold hierarchical structure in the Church: bishops, presbyters and deacons. While en route to Rome to become "food for wild animals because of his testimony to Christ,"[8] Ignatius composed letters to the Churches in Asia Minor and Rome. The first to use the term "Catholic Church" to mean the orthodox Christians collectively, he exhorts the faithful to obedience to their bishops: "Where the bishop [episkopos] appears, there let the people be, just as where Jesus Christ is, there is the Catholic Church."[9] The bishop is the responsible teacher of the faithful. To hold communion with him is to be protected from error and heresy. "Surely," he tells the Philadelphians, "all those who belong to God and Jesus Christ are the very ones who side with the bishop."[10] In this as in his other letters, Ignatius urges the faithful not to act independently of the bishop. Communion with the Church's officeholders guarantees the unity and peace which Christ wills for His followers. "He that does anything apart from bishop, presbyter or deacon, has no pure conscience."[11]

---

[8] Eusebius, Hist. eccl. 3.36.

[9] Smyrn. 8.2; cf. St. Cyril of Jerusalem, Catechesis 18.1: "the holy catholic Church" (PG 33, 1017a). St. Cyprian, too, uses "catholic" as the equivalent of "orthodox" (e.g., Epist. 73.2).

[10] Phld. 3; PG 5, 699. Similarly: "Subject yourselves to the bishop as Christ according to His human nature was subject to the Father and the apostles to Christ" (Magn. 13.2; PG 5, 674).

[11] Trall. 7.2; cf. Eph. 4.

By the second century, at least in the Churches addressed by Ignatius, the role of bishop and the role of celebrant of the Eucharist were joined. Only the bishop and delegated presbyters could preside over the Eucharistic liturgy.[12] The faithful were to manifest and foster communion with their bishop and presbyters by celebrating the Eucharist with them: "One Eucharist, one body of the Lord, one cup, one altar, and one bishop together with the presbyterium and the deacons."[13]

For Ignatius, as for the Apostle Paul, ecclesial communion has its source and supreme expression in the celebration of the Eucharist, which unites Christ the Head to each member of His Body the Church (1 Cor 10:17: "Because there is one bread, we who are many are one body, for we all partake of the one bread"). The Church is essentially a Eucharistic society. Her bishops (and presbyters) receive the imposition of hands, which has been handed down uninterruptedly from the first apostles, hearing and repeating the words that those apostles heard and repeated: *Do this in remembrance of Me.* The Church produces the Eucharist; in its turn, the Eucharist realizes the Church, in the strictest sense of the word. The apostolic succession is ordained to, and ensures the integrity of, the Eucharist.

No less important than communion with the local bishop is communion with the Bishop of Rome, for the Roman Church "presides in love" over the other Churches.[14] If communion with the bishop signifies and preserves the unity of the Church at the local level, the communion of the local Churches with one another and with the Church at Rome ensures the peace and unity of the universal Church.

In summary, we have seen that by the early-second century

---

[12] *Smyrn.* 8.1.
[13] *Phld.* 4.1; cf. *Eph.* 20.2 and *Smyrn.* 8.1.
[14] *Rom.* 1.1.

the names and functions of *episkopos*, presbyter and deacon have acquired sharper definition. At least in Syria and Asia Minor, each local Church was governed by a monarchical bishop who, as vicar of the true and only Priest, was high-priest of the Eucharistic liturgy. Beneath the presbyters were the deacons, "entrusted with the ministry of Jesus Christ,"[15] who looked after certain liturgical functions and performed charitable ministries. Once more, apostolicity is bound to catholicity, which entails communion with the Roman Church founded by the Apostle Peter and consecrated by his blood. In the words of the Roman liturgy, it is only "*una cum famulo tuo Papa nostro…*" ("together with Thy servant … our Pope"),[16] that the local Church makes present the Catholic and Apostolic Church.

### 2.3. The Didache

The oldest non-biblical document that we know is the anonymous *Didache* ("The Lord's Instruction to the Gentiles through the Twelve Apostles"), which was valued so highly by the early Christians that it nearly made its way into the New Testament. Strangely enough, it disappeared and became available only after its publication in 1883, eight years after its discovery in a manuscript, now in Jerusalem, dated 1056. The *Didache* is a collection of Church regulations written probably in Syria not later than the reign of Emperor Hadrian (117-38) and possibly even earlier. It speaks of the *episkopoi* and *diakonoi* as leaders of the local Churches, but says nothing of *presbuteroi* or of succession by the laying-on of hands:

> Accordingly, elect for yourselves bishops and deacons, men who are an honor to the Lord, of gentle disposition, not attached to money, honest and well-tried; for they, too, ren-

---

[15] *Magn.* 6.1.

[16] Roman Missal, Eucharistic Prayer I (Roman Canon).

der you the sacred service of the prophets and teachers. Do not, then, despise them; for they are your dignitaries together with the prophets and teachers.[17]

The author evidently feared that the local office-bearers might not receive the same respect as the itinerant prophets, who were greatly esteemed. The prophets were not to be criticized (11.7); they were judged by God alone (11.11). As "high priests" (*archieris*, 13.3) they were permitted (perhaps) even to celebrate the Eucharist (*eucharistein*, 10.7 — although some scholars think that this passage refers to the *agapé* fellowship meal).[18] During this early period, as one historian has noted, "the pneumatic-charismatic and the official-sacramental conceptions are here still co-existing without great difficulty."[19]

The exact history of the transition in Church leadership from apostles and prophets to *episkopoi* and deacons — a change reflected in *Didache* 15 (quoted above) — is shrouded in obscurity. For a generation or more, the apostles and prophets coexisted with the local ministry of bishops and deacons. What we do not know for certain is whether the charismatic prophets and certain others were believed to possess sacramental powers. Clearly for Ignatius, as we saw, the only valid (*bebaia*) Eucharist is that which is offered by a bishop or his appointee.[20] But in Ignatius we do not find the terminological precision between "valid" and "licit" that is available

[17] *Didache* 15.1-2; Quasten, 1:33-34.

[18] Quasten, 1:34; cf. Brown, *Priest and Bishop*, 19.

[19] Hans von Campenhausen, *Ecclesiastical Authority and Spiritual Power in the Church of the First Three Centuries*, trans. J.A. Baker (Palo Alto, Calif.: Stanford University Press, 1969), 177. Cf. Vorgrimler, 250-51 (with bibliography).
An interesting addition to the debate on office in the early Church is James T. Burtchaell, *From Synagogue to Church* (New York: Cambridge University, 1992). Burtchaell argues that office-bearers presided over the Christian community from the beginning of the Church, but frequently deferred leadership to more charismatic members.

[20] *Smyrn.* 8.2.

today; hence we cannot be certain if he intended to say that nothing happens sacramentally to the bread and wine used in unauthorized liturgies.

Whatever the case, more or less contemporaneous with the *Didache* was the emergence of a strong consciousness of the institutional and historical aspects of the Church, partly in response to the swelling of congregations and partly in response to heresy and sectarianism (as we shall see with St. Irenaeus). Hence the instruction (15.1), in connection with other instructions on holding Eucharist (14), to appoint bishops and deacons. From this period onward, Eucharistic presidency would be restricted to the bishop and his fellow presbyters.

## 2.4. St. Irenaeus of Lyons

Throughout the second century, Gnosticism posed a lethal threat to the apostolic faith (1 Tm 6:20: "what is falsely called knowledge [*gnôsis*]").[21] Rejecting the Church's faith, the Gnostics claimed to possess a more perfect knowledge of divine revelation through a secret tradition to which only they had access. Ignorance of this *gnôsis*, and not sin, is responsible for human suffering and alienation from God. The apocryphal *Apocalypse of Peter* establishes the Apostle Peter as the foundation of Gnostic revelation and impugns the Church hierarchy as "dry canals" who persecute the Gnostic elect.[22] Thus it is easy to understand why Gnostics spurned the apostolic Tradition and its official custodians, the successors

---

[21] For a good overview of Gnosticism, see the *New Jerome Biblical Commentary*, ed. Raymond E. Brown, S.S., Joseph A. Fitzmyer, S.J. and Roland E. Murphy, O.Carm. (Englewood Cliffs, N.J.: Prentice Hall, Inc., 1990), 1350-53; also, Henry Chadwick, *The Early Church*, vol. 1 of the *Penguin History of the Church*, gen. ed. Owen Chadwick (London: Pelican Books, 1967; repr. New York: Viking Penguin, 1990), 33-41. A more exhaustive study is Kurt Rudolf, *Gnosis: The Nature and History of Gnosticism* (New York: Harper & Row, 1987).

[22] *Apoc. Pet.* 79.22 — 80.7.

of the apostles. After all, those who have private access to divine secrets are in no need of unenlightened teachers.

Irenaeus (ca. 140 - 202), bishop of Lyons, met the Gnostic challenge and earned renown as the greatest orthodox theologian of his day. There is no secret tradition in the Church, a kind of esoteric doctrine, communicated only to the initiated. Whoever wishes to know the truth must look at the Tradition of the apostles, which is public and demonstrable even to the simplest.[23] The original Christian message is found in the Church, where it is handed down from generation to generation equally to one and all. Its basis is Scripture, read in the light of the Church's Tradition of worship and teaching. The best proof that Christians possess the original teaching of the apostles lies in the communities whose leaders can be traced back to the apostles. The unbroken succession of bishops in the great dioceses founded by the apostles guarantees the integrity and purity of Tradition. In his famous treatise, *Against the Heresies* (ca. 185), in which he refutes all the erroneous teachings of his day, Irenaeus writes:

> Anyone who wishes to discern the truth may see in every Church in the whole world the apostolic Tradition clear and manifest. We can enumerate those who were appointed as bishops in the Churches by the apostles and their successors to our own day, who never knew and never taught anything resembling their [= the Gnostics'] foolish doctrine. Had the apostles known any such mysteries, which they taught privately and *sub rosa* to the perfect, they would surely have entrusted this teaching to the men in whose charge they placed the Churches. For they wished them to be without blame and reproach to whom they handed over their own position of authority.[24]

---

[23] "The Apostolic Faith has no secrets, no inner light reserved for a brightened few; the last book of the Scriptures is Revelation, with all its seven seals open." George William Rutler, *Saint John Vianney: The Curé d'Ars Today* (San Francisco: Ignatius, 1988), 106.

[24] *Adv. Hær.* 3.3.1; Quasten, 1:301.

Irenaeus adds that, even if the apostles had not left us Scripture, the apostolic Tradition would have been enough for our instruction and salvation.[25]

How can one know whether a congregation professes the authentic Christian faith, uncorrupted by error? Orthodox Christianity is apostolic Christianity and nothing else. Any other "gospel" is *anathema* (cf. 2 Cor 11:4; Gal 1:6-9). They are not true Christians whose exotic brand of "Christianity" is founded, not on the Tradition of the apostles, but on the *gnôsis* of an elite few who boast of themselves as "improvers of the apostles."[26] The apostolic Tradition *is* orthodoxy, and the apostolic succession is its form and confirmation.

Elsewhere in his treatise, Irenaeus writes:

> It is necessary to obey the presbyters in the Church, those who, as we have shown, have succession from the apostles, those who have received, with the succession of the episcopate, the sure [*certum*] charism of truth according to the good pleasure of the Father.

By contrast with the Christian authority of those presbyters with *episcopê*, "others who are outside the original succession, and hold their meetings in holes and corners, we must treat with suspicion."[27]

Like Ignatius of Antioch, Irenaeus greatly esteemed the Roman Church as the channel of pure apostolic doctrine. After enumerating the Roman bishops up to Pope St. Eleutherus (ca. 174-89), he goes on to say:

> In this order and by this succession, the ecclesiastical Tradition from the apostles and the preaching of the truth have

---

[25] *Ibid.* 3.4.1.
[26] *Ibid.* 3.3.1.
[27] *Ibid.* 4.26.2.

come down to us. And this is most abundant proof that there is one and the same vivifying faith which the Church has received from the apostles, preserved until now, and handed down in truth.[28]

Rome exercises a special ministry of unity, so that the bishops and all the faithful may be undivided:

> For every Church must be in harmony with this Church [= Rome] because of its outstanding pre-eminence [*potentiorem principalitatem*], that is, the faithful from everywhere [must be in harmony with this Church], since the apostolic Tradition is preserved in it by those from everywhere.[29]

## 2.5. Tertullian

Although technically he was not a Father of the Church, the brilliant African orator Tertullian of Carthage (ca. 160 - ca. 225) bore strong witness to the necessity of the apostolic succession. In his most valuable treatise, *The Prescription of Heretics* (ca. 200), composed before he left the Catholic Church in favor of Montanism, Tertullian writes:

> Their [= all heretics'] doctrine, after comparison with that of the apostles, will declare, by its own diversity and contrariety, that it had for its author neither an apostle nor an apostolic man; because, as the apostles would never have taught things which were self-contradictory, so the apostolic men would not have inculcated teaching different from

---

[28] *Ibid.* 3.3.3; Quasten, 1:303.

[29] *Ibid.* 3.3.2. The original Greek text of this passage is unavailable. Quasten notes (1:302-03) that *potentiorem principalitatem* could be translated, "superior origin," referring to the founders, Peter and Paul (so D. van den Eynde and G. Bardy); or, "more efficient leadership" (so A. Ehrhard). Whatever the case, it is with the Roman Church that all Churches must be in accord, because Rome has preserved apostolic Tradition in its fullness.

the apostles. To this test, therefore, will the heretics be sub-
mitted for proof by those Churches who, although they
derive not their founder from an apostle or apostolic man
(as being of much later date, for in fact they are being
founded daily); yet, since they agree in the same faith, they
are accounted as not less apostolic, because they are akin in
doctrine.[30]

In Tertullian's mind, a new community with no formal link
to the apostles could be recognized as apostolic just the same, provided it hold the same faith (*eadem fide*) as the existing apostolic
Churches. If we isolate this passage, Tertullian seemed concerned
more with the message or "content" of Tradition (*what* is taught)
than with its messenger or "form" (*who* is teaching): it is enough
to be "akin in doctrine" (*consanguinitate doctrinæ*) with the other
Churches. His concern for doctrinal succession is appreciated. A
bishop who falls away from the faith of the apostles is no longer
useful to the Church, and has in fact become her enemy. Even so,
it is worth asking: how can we know that the message professed is
the authentic Tradition? Why should *this* messenger be believed,
but not *that* one? Why Ignatius or Irenaeus, but not Basilides or
Marcion?

In an earlier passage, Tertullian noted that the bishops were
the original "heirs" of apostolic doctrine and therefore could attest
to it in all the Churches.[31] A fair reading of Tertullian acknowledges his balanced position: whereas the apostolic faith forms the
content of the apostolic succession, the apostolic succession in authority passes on and guarantees the authenticity of the message.
Authority is at once "form" (the exercise of office) and proclaimed
"content" (the Gospel). The apostolic Church is found where both
apostolic teaching and apostolic authority exist.

---

[30] *De Præscriptione hæreticorum* 32; PL 2, 45.
[31] *Ibid.* 20; PL 2, 31.

## 2.6. Clement of Alexandria

The unfinished *Stromata* (literally, "tapestries") of Clement of Alexandria (ca. 150 - ca. 215), a Christian philosopher-theologian whose biography is practically unknown, provides a very interesting contrast to the writings of Irenaeus and Tertullian. Clement takes up the objection raised against Christianity by the existence of so many competing sects. Gnosticism had made philosophy suspect; but Clement saw in philosophy a rational method for the refutation of Gnostic heresies and for the support of orthodoxy, and so did not hesitate to use the language of philosophy and even of Gnosticism and the mystery cults. For Clement, true *gnôsis* is faith in divine revelation, strengthened and perfected by reflection and synthesis.

Whereas for Irenaeus and Tertullian the historical episcopacy makes present the apostolic Tradition, for Clement it is the true Christian gnostic that constitutes Tradition. Nowhere in his writings against the heretical Gnostics does Clement refer to the contemporary bishop of Alexandria, Demetrius, or to the whole episcopate as the prime guarantor of apostolicity. Those who devote their lives to understanding "the prophets, the gospel, and the blessed apostles" are the surest guides to truth.[32] Thus if we would talk about the idea of apostolic succession in Clement, we should ascribe it to those teachers who make up for the absence of the apostles by their study and teaching — a succession of doctrine rather than a succession of bishops:

> Those, then, also now, who have exercised themselves in the Lord's commandments, and lived perfectly and gnostically according to the Gospel, may be enrolled in the chosen body of the apostles. Such an one is in reality a presbyter of the

---

[32] *Stromata* 7.16.

Church, and true minister (deacon) of the will of God, if
he do and teach what is the Lord's; not as being ordained
by men, nor regarded righteous because a presbyter, but
enrolled in the presbyterate because righteous. And although
here upon earth he be not honored with the chief seat, he
will sit down on the four-and-twenty thrones, judging the
people, as John says in the Apocalypse.[33]

Where Clement does mention the Church hierarchy, it is to parallel the three grades of Order with the angelic hierarchy:

According to my opinion the grades here in the Church of
bishops, priests and deacons are imitations of the angelic
glory and of that economy which, the Scriptures say, awaits
those who following the footsteps of the apostles, "have lived
in perfection of righteousness according to the Gospel."[34]

Thus with Clement of Alexandria we find in Tradition some pre-
cedent for the characteristically Protestant stress on doctrinal succession or "content."

### 2.7. St. Cyprian of Carthage

Much has been said about the importance of holding communion with the bishop: in doing so, one belongs to Christ and is
safeguarded from error and heresy. "You should understand," coun-
sels Cyprian, the martyred bishop of Carthage (ca. 205-258), "that
the bishop is in the Church and the Church in the bishop, and that
whoever is not with the bishop is not in the Church."[35] The criterion of Church membership is no longer, as for Clement of Alexandria, mere acceptance of the doctrines guaranteed by the episco-

---

[33] *Ibid.* 6.13.
[34] *Ibid.*
[35] *Epist.* 66.8; Quasten, *Patrology*, vol. 2, *The Ante-Nicene Literature After Irenaeus*
(Utrecht: Spectrum, 1950; reprint, Westminster, Md.: Christian Classics, Inc, 1992),
374.

pate as apostolic, but submission to the bishop himself. Cyprian writes of the antipope Novatian: "We are not interested in what he teaches, since he teaches outside the Church. Whatever and whatsoever kind of man he is, he is not a Christian who is not in Christ's Church."[36] Rebellion against the bishop is rebellion against God.[37]

The communion of the bishops among themselves is no less important, since it is due to this communion that all the local Churches make up the one Catholic Church. Were a congregation to depart from this communion, it would immediately cease to exist as Church. This is the theme of Cyprian's treatise *On the Unity of the Church*. Christ founded His Church upon the Apostle Peter. To be a Christian means to remain in this one Church, the spiritual home of the faithful.

> The Lord speaks to Peter, saying, "I say unto thee, that thou art Peter; and upon this rock I will build My Church, and the gates of hell shall not prevail against it..." [Mt 16:18]. And although to all the apostles, after His resurrection, He gives an equal power, and says, "As the Father hath sent Me, even so send I you: Receive the Holy Ghost: Whose soever sins ye remit, they shall be remitted unto him; and whose soever sins ye retain, they shall be retained" [Jn 20:21]; yet, that He might set forth unity, He arranged by His authority the origin of that unity, as beginning from one. Assuredly the rest of the apostles were also the same as was Peter, endowed with a like partnership both of honor and power; but the beginning proceeds from unity that the Church of Christ might be manifested to be one... Does he who does not hold to this unity of the Church think that he holds the faith? Does he who strives against and resists the Church trust that he is in the Church...?[38]

---

[36] *Epist.* 55.24; J.N.D. Kelly, *Early Christian Doctrines*, rev. ed. (San Francisco: Harper & Row, 1978), 206.

[37] *Epist.* 66.1.

[38] *De Unitate Ecclesiae* 4-5; Quasten, 2:350-51.

While Cyprian exalted the Roman Church as the "root and mother of the Catholic Church,"[39] his words should not be taken as a recognition of the Bishop of Rome's universal jurisdiction over every Church. "So long as the bond of friendship is maintained and the sacred unity of the Catholic Church is preserved, each bishop is master of his own conduct" and answerable to God alone.[40] But Cyprian did not disregard episcopal collegiality. Each bishop is seen in reference to his fellow bishops: he and they together form one episcopate only.[41] The Catholic Church is constituted locally (as Ignatius saw) by the faithful in communion with their bishop and celebrating the Eucharist; and she is constituted universally by the communion of the bishops of the local Churches with one another and with the Bishop of Rome, who is the successor of St. Peter and the visible center of Catholic truth and unity. The bishop who is in communion with the Bishop of Rome is *ipso facto* in communion with all the other bishops.

With Cyprian the distance, the key difference, between the apostles and the bishops disappears, so that the apostolate *is* the episcopate. The bishops are the successors of the apostles and the apostles were the bishops of old. "The Lord chose the apostles, that is, the bishops and rulers."[42] The Church is built upon them. This view is evident in the reckoning of Peter the first Bishop of Rome:

---

[39] *Epist.* 48.3; cf. 59.14

[40] *Epist.* 55.21 (PL 2, 348-49); cf. 60.3 (PL 4, 372). This is the ecclesiology of the Orthodox Church, which does not believe any bishop to be endowed with universal jurisdiction. The Bishop of Rome is "first among equals," and his primacy is one of honor and *agape*. Roman Catholicism and Eastern Orthodoxy differ over papal supremacy, not papal primacy.

[41] *De Unit.* 5: "One is the episcopate, whose part is held as a whole by each and every one; one is the Church, which is extended into a wider multitude by an increase of fecundity." Cf. St. Cyril of Alexandria (PG 77, 293); Pope St. Celestine I (PL 50, 505-11).

[42] *Epist.* 3.3.; cf. 66.4; 75.16.

Our Lord, Whose commandment we must fear and obey, establishes the honorable rank of bishop and the constitution of His Church when in the gospel He speaks and says to Peter: "I say to thee: Thou art Peter and upon this rock I will build my Church and the gates of hell shall not prevail against it. And I will give to thee the keys of the kingdom of heaven. And whatsoever thou shalt bind on earth, it shall be bound also in heaven, and whatsoever thou shalt loose on earth, it shall be loosed also in heaven" [Mt 16:18 f.]. Thence have come down to us in the course of time and by due succession the ordained office of the bishop and the constitution of the Church, forasmuch as the Church is founded upon the bishops and every act of the Church is subject to these rulers.[43]

## Summary

We have seen different ecclesiastical writers stress different aspects of the apostolic succession. With St. Clement of Rome at the end of the first century, there is the *principle* of succession going back to the mind of the apostles and, behind them, to Christ. In the late-second century, we find St. Irenaeus and Tertullian testifying to the important interplay between orthodox doctrine and legitimate office. On the one hand, legitimate appointment is indispensable to the apostolic succession. Here Tertullian is eloquent against the heretics: "Let them unfold the series of their bishops..." On the other hand, without orthodox teaching, succession ceases or never really begins. Irenaeus expresses this constantly: the bishops in apostolic succession "never knew and have never taught" Gnosticism's weird doctrines. Furthermore, there is specifically *doctrinal* succession, the succession of Christian teachers, whether

---

[43] *Epist.* 33.1; Quasten, 2:374-75.

they be bishops or not. In this area Clement of Alexandria comes on strong.

By the mid-third century, the difference between the apostles and the bishops disappears with Cyprian. The bishops are not merely in succession *from* the apostles, but are the successors *of* the apostles. There is a general consensus that the office of bishop is of divine origin. But we have also noted that it is not until St. Ignatius of Antioch that we find: a lucid distinction between *episkopoi* and *presbuteroi*; one *episkopos* presiding over each local Church, standing out clearly from the local presbyterate (at least in the Churches of Syria and Asia Minor); and the transition from collegial ministry in local Churches to a more clearly delineated three-ordered hierarchy.

In the minds of the early Fathers, apostolicity was understood as succession both of apostolic doctrine (what Irenaeus termed the "canon of truth") *and* of apostolic men. A Church's claim to orthodoxy is generally substantiated by its apostolic origin, by its ordained ministers standing in historical succession to the apostles. From earliest times, Christians recognized the presbyter-*episkopoi* as successors of the apostles, with the special responsibility for safeguarding and handing on the apostolic Tradition. Succession in office, the Church's Tradition and sacramental-juridical communion are not juxtaposed, but "triune." A congregation may not encapsulate itself from the other Churches. If it should do so, it would cease to be Church and would soon fracture. Catholicity preserves and expresses apostolicity.[44]

---

[44] Cf. Joseph Ratzinger, *Introduction to Christianity*, trans. J.R. Foster (San Francisco: Ignatius Press, 1990), 266-68. (Originally published in German as *Einführung in das Christentum* [Munich: Kösel-Verlag GmbH & Co., 1968].)

Chapter Three

# The Liturgical Expression of Apostolicity

The Catholic understanding of the liturgy is summarized in the ancient maxim, *Lex orandi, lex credendi*: the norm of prayer establishes the norm of belief, and *vice versa*.[1] The Church's liturgy is the most important public repository of the truths which she professes and the symbols that teach those truths. If it is in the liturgy where the Christian comes into direct contact with the apostolic Tradition, then our study of the apostolic succession cannot afford to overlook the *lex orandi*.

## 3.1. The rite of ordination described by St. Hippolytus of Rome

Especially useful to us is *The Apostolic Tradition* of the Roman presbyter Hippolytus (martyred 235), a disciple of Irenaeus. Written about 215, *The Apostolic Tradition* is, "with the exception of the *Didache*, the earliest and the most important of the ancient Christian Church orders...."[2] The first part contains, among other things,

---

[1] This axiom is attested in the fifth-century *Indiculus de gratia Dei* (DS 246).

[2] Quasten, 2:180. The original Greek text of this document is lost but for some fragments in later Greek documents, especially in the eighth book of the *Apostolic Constitutions*, which became the basis for ordination liturgies in the Christian East. Translations of the *Apostolic Tradition* are available in Latin, Arabic, Coptic and Ethiopic. "The combination of them," Quasten notes (pg. 181), "enables us to get an adequate perception of its actual wording and the tenor of the entire document."

prayers for the ordination of bishops, presbyters and deacons, and the Eucharistic liturgy following thereon, including liturgical rubrics. Although *The Apostolic Tradition* was not the official liturgical book of the Roman Church, the Anglican historian of liturgy, Dom Gregory Dix, assures us: "We may safely take it that in outline and essentials the rites and customs to which *The Apostolic Tradition* bears witness were those practiced in the Roman Church in his [= Hippolytus'] day, and in his own youth ca. A.D. 180."[3]

According to Hippolytus, the ordination of a bishop occurs on a Sunday after he has been "chosen by all the people" and in the most public manner possible. At least two or three bishops are to attend, and the presbyters are to be present, together with the whole congregation. The bishops are to lay their hands upon the elected man, the presbyters standing by in silence. All are to keep silent, praying for the coming of the Holy Spirit. Then one of the bishops, "at the request of all," lays hands on the ordinand's head and prays aloud:

"O God and Father of our Lord Jesus Christ, Father of mercies and God of all comfort," "Who dwellest on high yet hast respect unto the lowly," "Who knowest all things before they come to pass";

Who didst give ordinances unto Thy Church "by the Word of Thy grace"; Who "didst foreordain from the beginning" the race of the righteous from Abraham, instituting princes and priests and leaving not Thy sanctuary without ministers; Who from the foundation of the world hast been pleased to be glorified in them whom Thou hast chosen:

… now pour forth that Power which is from Thee, of "the princely Spirit" which Thou didst deliver to Thy Beloved Child Jesus Christ, which He bestowed on Thy holy apostles

[3] Gregory Dix, O.S.B., ed., *The Treatise on the Apostolic Tradition of Hippolytus of Rome* (London: SPCK, 1937), xxxix-xl.

who established the Church which hallows Thee in every place to the endless glory and praise of Thy Name.

Father, "Who knowest the hearts of all," grant upon this Thy servant whom Thou hast chosen for the episcopate to feed Thy holy flock and serve as Thine high priest, that he may minister blamelessly by night and day, that he may unceasingly behold and propitiate Thy countenance and offer to Thee the gifts of Thy holy Church.

And that by the high-priestly Spirit he may have authority "to forgive sins" according to Thy command, "to assign lots" according to Thy bidding, to "loose every bond" according to the authority Thou gavest to the apostles, and that he may please Thee in meekness and a pure heart, "offering to Thee a sweet smelling savour,"

through Thy Child Jesus Christ our Lord, through Whom to Thee be glory, might and praise, to the Father and to the Son with the Holy Spirit now and ever and world without end. Amen.[4]

This earliest ordination prayer is essentially an *epiklêsis*, a prayer for the descent of the Holy Spirit upon the candidate, to enable him to fulfill his priestly, prophetic and kingly *munera*. It is the "governing Spirit" (*to hêgêmonikon Pneuma*, which Dix renders as "princely") Whom, so the prayer reads, the Father gave to the Son, and the Son to the apostles.

It can hardly be doubted that this prayer expresses the conviction that the mandate which Jesus gave to His apostles, and the authority which He gave them to carry it out, continued to exist in the Church, maintained from generation to generation in the body of men ordained to the episcopate.[5]

---

[4] Hippolytus, *Traditio apostolica* 1.2-4; Dix's edition, 3.

[5] Francis A. Sullivan, S.J., *The Church We Believe In: One, Holy, Catholic and Apostolic* (New York: Paulist Press, 1988), 178.

A comparison with the prayers for the ordination of a presbyter and of a deacon shows that in each case the words that qualify the Spirit that is to be given are appropriate to the kind of ministry the ordinand will have. Thus, for the presbyter, the ordaining bishop prays that the Father would impart "the Spirit of grace and counsel," while for the deacon he asks "the Spirit of grace and earnestness and diligence."

What kind of ministry is the bishop to exercise? He is to be an authoritative leader. The word *hēgoumenôn*, a cognate of "princely," is used in the Letter to the Hebrews in reference to the "leaders" (living and deceased) of the community to whom the letter is addressed (Heb 13:7, 17, 24). The bishop is also to "serve as high priest," to act as a middleman between God and the Church. He alone is explicitly described as a priest, with the power (*exousia*) to forgive sins and to loose every bond. The term "priest" (Greek *hierus*; Latin *sacerdos*) began to be used for the bishop in the second century, because he presided at the Eucharist.

The rite of episcopal ordination recorded by Hippolytus is profoundly *Christological*. The Father has given full authority to the Son, Who in turn bestowed spiritual power and authority on the apostles. Ordination links the new bishop to Christ, the Father's Son and Apostle (Heb 3:1), the ultimate Source of authority in the Church.

Bishops are to be ordained only by other bishops; it was only in this way that a man could have a part in the apostolic mandate which had been handed down from the apostles, who themselves received it from the Lord Jesus. The bishop, then, stands in direct relationship to Jesus as His ambassador, such that his succession in office does not essentially mean origin from the apostles, but more importantly origin from the Lord Jesus.[6]

---

[6] Kenan B. Osborne, O.F.M., *Priesthood: A History of the Ordained Ministry in the Roman Catholic Church* (New York: Paulist Press, 1988), 81.

The rite is *pneumatological* as well as Christological; for this prayer is basically an *epiklēsis*, a calling-down of the Holy Spirit onto the candidate. The laying-on of hands, which is a sacramental sign of the Spirit's "descent," must be associated with prayer. The ordaining bishop did not confer the Spirit. He had to beseech the Father to send Him, confident that the Father, "Who knowest the hearts of all," has called the ordinand to the episcopate. Only after receiving the high-priestly Spirit (*to archieratikon Pneuma*) can the bishop exercise his sacred ministry. Forgiving sins, assigning lots, loosing bonds — these are, after all, God's work. And it is only in the Holy Spirit — without Whom we cannot even be moved to pray — that the prayers of the Church ascend to the Triune God as a "sweet-smelling savour."

Furthermore, the ordination rite is *ecclesiological*. The candidate must have been selected by the congregation, clergy and people together, and "found acceptable by all."[7] His commission is a charism given to him for self-sacrificing service to the people of God. In the presence of the community, and at their request, one of the bishops imposes hands on him. Because the episcopate is collegial in character, the consecration of a new bishop is carried out by at least two bishops, never by one alone.[8] The new bishop is made a fellow member of the college of bishops. The juridical communion existing among the Catholic episcopate makes it possible for the ordinand to become a successor of the apostles. Immediately following the ordination, the kiss of peace is given and the presbyters join their new bishop in the celebration of the Eucharist, which is the foundation of the Church's unity.

---

[7] With the advent of a Christian emperor in the fourth century it became common for the bishops of the principal cities in Christendom to be imperially nominated.

[8] After the Synod of Arles in 314 and the Council of Nicaea in 325, the consecration of a bishop must be carried out by three bishops.

## 3.2. Other sources

While prayer and the laying-on of hands formed the heart of the ordination rite, still it is worth asking whether there were other means of ordination in the early Church. In the first three centuries of the Church, the "imposition of hands" could also describe a simple selection or choice; similarly, *ordinare* could retain the meaning of "appoint" or "designate."[9] Arnold Ehrhardt accepts the imposition of hands as the normal mode of entry into Church office, but points out that

> it was, however, the enthronement which seems to have been regarded by the Pseudo-Clementines as the constitutive act. This view is supported by the claim that the original chair of St. James had been preserved at Jerusalem; and this is also the reason why Rome made a similar claim in respect to the chair of St. Peter...[10]

The "Father of Church History," Eusebius Pamphili, bishop of Caesarea in Palestine until his death in 339, regularly refers to the "episcopal throne" of Jerusalem (and of nowhere else), and tells us that it still existed in his day.[11] In Books II-VII of his ten-volume *Church History*, Eusebius lists the succession of bishops in the four principal sees of the Church: Rome, Alexandria, Antioch and Jerusalem.

Some authors conjecture that there were two standard forms of installation to the monepiscopate which were standard in the second century: an enthronement, reflected in the early references to the *cathedra*, and the imposition of hands. Presumably, then, either form could have constituted episcopal consecration.[12] However, given the solid biblical and apostolic foundations for the laying-on of hands, it

---

[9] Vorgrimler, 252.

[10] Arnold Ehrhardt, *The Apostolic Succession in the First Two Centuries of the Church* (London: Lutterworth Press, 1953), 82.

[11] *Hist. eccl.* 7.19.

[12] Osborne, 120. With regard to the enthroning rite, he cites D. Dupuy, "Theologie der kirchlichen Ämter," *Mysterium Salutis* 4, no. 2 (Einsiedeln: Benzinger, 1973): 503.

does not seem reckless to suppose that enthronement always followed
sacramental ordination by the imposition of hands and an accompanying prayer, as is the procedure today.[13] At any rate, if there were
no imposition of hands in some places, the gesture was no doubt universally standard by the time of St. Jerome, whose commentary on
the Book of Isaiah (ca. 409) uses the term *ordinatio* as a synonym for
the Greek *cheirôtonia*, the laying-on of hands.[14]

The ancient professions of faith, or creeds, provide us with
another liturgical witness of the Church's own understanding of her
apostolicity. The term "apostolic" made a late entrance into the official Christian creeds. The baptismal creed of the Western Church
— the so-called "Apostles' Creed" — mentions only two attributes
of the Church: "holy" and "catholic."[15] Around the mid-fourth century, the baptismal creed in use at Jerusalem, as we know from St.
Cyril's *Catecheses*, described the Church as "one, holy and catholic."[16]

The first baptismal creed in which the attribute "apostolic"
appears is the one that was in use in the Church at Salamis (Con-
stantia), on the Eastern Mediterranean island of Cyprus, after the
mid-fourth century. The text of this creed is found in the *Ancoratus*
(literally, *The Firmly-Anchored Man*), a compendium of Christian
doctrine written in 374 by St. Epiphanius, bishop of Salamis.[17] The
Council of Constantinople (381) accepted this profession of faith with
a few modifications, thereby establishing it as the baptismal creed
throughout the Christian East. What we now refer to as the
Niceno-Constantinopolitan Creed was eventually incorporated into
the Eucharistic liturgy, first in the East, then much later (and in
slightly different form) in the West.

---

[13] Cf. *Ceremonial of Bishops* (Collegeville, MN: Liturgical Press, 1989), no. 1138:
enthronement follows episcopal ordination.
[14] *Commentarium in Isaiam* 16.58.10; PL 24, 569.
[15] DS 30.
[16] *Catechesis* 18; PG 33, 1043-50; DS 41.
[17] PG 43, 232; DS 42. A second and longer creed, composed by Epiphanius himself,
follows thereafter (DS 44-45).

*Summary*

Let us summarize what has been said up to now. From the Resurrection and Ascension of Jesus to the beginning of the third century, the history of the ordination rite is sketchy. Only in the *Apostolic Tradition* of St. Hippolytus do we find an ordination ceremony clearly explained. Hippolytus provides us with a most reliable witness to the doctrine and practice of the ante-Nicene Church. The laying-on of hands would come to be regarded as the normal method of ordination in the Church. The gesture is biblical, being associated with a long and venerable tradition associated with Moses (Dt 34:9; Nb 27:23) and "Christianized" by Jesus' apostles and their auxiliaries (Ac 6:5-6; 8:17; 13:2-3; 14:23; 19:5; 1 Tm 4:14; 2 Tm 1:6).

Passing on the apostolic ministry presupposed hierarchical communion among the bishops of the universal Church. This communion was made vividly manifest at episcopal consecrations, when the bishops of different particular Churches within the universal Church would come together to impose hands on the ordinand in the presence of the whole local congregation. The bishop does not receive his authority from the community or from the collegial body of presbyters. Rather, his authority comes directly from God.

Not until relatively late (the fourth century) does the attribute "apostolic" occur in the Church's liturgical creeds. As far as we know, the first time the term appears alongside the other attributes of the Church is in the baptismal creed introduced at Salamis (in Cyprus) shortly before the election of St. Epiphanius as bishop of that metropolitan see. The Council of Constantinople, held in 381, endorsed this creed, making it the standard profession of faith throughout Eastern Christendom. Gradually, the Niceno-Constantinopolitan Creed was adopted in the West. Consequently, all orthodox Christians came to profess faith in Christ's Church as "one, holy, catholic and apostolic."

Chapter Four

# From Antiquity to the Protestant Reformation

The vast span of Church history from the early patristic period to the Protestant Reformation saw considerable theological development with regard to the sacrament of Order: its purpose, its quality or "character," why it is a sacrament, of how many degrees it consists, who is its proper minister, and so on. It is not our aim to trace the history of thought on the sacrament of Order. Rather, the questions relating to Order will be considered only so far as they relate specifically to the apostolic succession.

The controversy in the fourth century concerning whether or not there are sacraments outside the Church is important, of course, because Order is one of the sacraments. If the sacraments of heretics and schismatics are null and void, then there is no apostolic succession outside the Church's visible unity, and this book would not have been written. From this debate, we move on to the late Middle Ages, where we find the requirements for sacramental validity spelled out. Tangential to the apostolic succession are the questions, left unresolved until quite recently, regarding the nature of the episcopate (how is it differentiated from the presbyterate?) and the rite of ordination (what constitutes the gesture or "matter" of Order?). With the Protestant Reformation at the end of the medieval period, the whole identity of the Church was called into question: what and where is the Church?

## 4.1. Sacraments outside the Church? Augustine vs. Cyprian

Half a century after St. Cyprian's martyrdom in 258, North African Christians were split between two rival communities, Catholic and Donatist.[1] Both sides affirmed the same creeds and claimed to be the *ecclesia catholica*, the one catholic Church and ark of salvation. The schism divided African Christians for a century, and survived until Catholic and Donatist alike were swept away by Islam.

Donatism (named after Donatus, bishop of Numidia) evidently originated in fierce opposition to the consecration of Caecilian as bishop of Carthage in 311. The Donatists accused one of Caecilian's consecrators of having surrendered copies of the Bible, liturgical books and sacred vessels to the civil authorities during the Diocletian persecution in 303. To Donatists this was apostasy pure and simple, an affront to the glorious witness of those Christians who chose death over surrender. Caecilian and his successors were contaminated by this moral and ritual impurity, as well as those who held ecclesiastical communion with them, including the Bishop of Rome. Hence, in Donatist eyes, the so-called Catholic Church could not possibly be the true Church which St. Paul described in Ephesians 5:27 as being without blemish or wrinkle.

The Donatists followed St. Cyprian in maintaining that the validity of the sacraments depends on the proper standing of the minister.[2] If someone loses the Spirit through grave sin (which includes heresy, schism and apostasy), then he cannot confer the Spirit's gifts, including Baptism. Accordingly, those who had been "baptized" outside the Church are reconciled to her by first receiv-

---

[1] For brief overviews of Donatism, see Kelly, *Early Christian Doctrines*, 410; also Chadwick, *The Early Church*, 219-25.

[2] Cyprian declared: "All heretics and schismatics fail to give the Holy Spirit," Epist. 76.10; PL 3, 1191-93.

ing what is not a second Baptism but a first. A modern Church historian remarks of Cyprian:

> If his doctrine seems harsh and legalist, it was only the ob-
> verse of his passionate conviction that the Church was the
> Body of Christ, pulsing with the life of the Spirit, and that
> to claim the grace of Christ and His Spirit outside its fron-
> tiers was at once presumptuous and illogical.[3]

Fundamental to Cyprian's position is the premise that the Church's apostolic commission authenticates the ministry of word and sacrament; hence, ordained ministers who leave the Church do not take valid sacraments with them. This remains the dominant theology of sacramental validity in Eastern Orthodoxy.

Nearly a century after Cyprian, whose doctrine gained currency throughout the region, another North African bishop was working out his own sacramental theology. St. Augustine of Hippo (354-430) followed the Roman tradition of Pope St. Stephen I, who in 256 had upheld against Cyprian the teaching that sacramental validity is independent of the moral and spiritual condition of the minister.[4] Augustine ascribed all sacramental acts, including schismatic ones, not to the minister but to Christ. Hence he opposed the rebaptism and reordination of schismatics who wished to be reconciled with the Catholic Church. Ironically, Augustine could recognize the validity of Donatist sacraments precisely because of his opposition to Cyprianic-Donatist theology.

But the sacraments of schismatics, though valid, are not fruit-

---

[3] Kelly, 207.

[4] Pope Stephen instructs Cyprian: "If, therefore, some come to you from any heresy whatsoever let no innovation be made except according to what has been handed down, namely, let an imposition of hands be made on them by way of penance; for the heretics themselves are right in not baptizing other heretics who come over to them but simply receiving them into their communion" (DS 110).

ful, since the Church is the Holy Spirit's dwelling. As Augustine insists:

> When a person is baptized in some heretical or schismatic group, outside the communion of the Church, his baptism is of no profit to him, inasmuch as he gives his consent to the perversity of those heretics or schismatics.[5]

The Donatists make their sacraments ineffectual by their lack of charity, by their separation from that communion in faith, hope and love which is the Church universal. The grace of their sacraments can be fully released only upon reconciling with the Catholic Church. It would seem, however, that Augustine did not regard the sacrament of Order conferred outside the visible unity of the Church as technically within the apostolic succession.[6] The Augustinian solution was so significant a turnabout in the ideas and practice hitherto prevalent, that it took nearly a millennium before the older, Cyprianic conceptions were finally supplanted in the Western Church.[7]

Under the influence of Aristotelian philosophy, the late medieval Scholastics greatly broadened out Augustine's sacramental theology. A sacrament, though "invalidly" administered (for example, by someone who lacks the power of Order), could nonetheless be received fruitfully — that is, as having the same saving

---

[5] *De baptismo* 3.10.13 (PL 43, 146); cf. 4.17.24 (PL 43, 170). Referring to a Donatist bishop, Augustine said: "Outside the Catholic Church he can have everything except salvation. He can have honor, he can have sacraments, he can sing alleluia, he can respond with Amen. He can have the gospel, he can hold and preach the faith in the Name of the Father and of the Son and of the Holy Spirit but nowhere else than in the Catholic Church can he find salvation" (*Sermo ad Cæs. eccl. pleb.* 6 [PL 43, 695]; cf. *De bapt.* 1.12.18 [PL 43, 119]).

[6] Cf. Cuthbert H. Turner, "Apostolic Succession," in *Essays on the Early History of the Church and the Ministry*, ed. H.B. Swete, 2nd ed. (London: Macmillan & Co., 1921), 145 ff.

[7] *Ibid.*, 170.

effects as a "validly" administered sacrament — provided the recipient have the desire (*votum*) to receive the grace of the sacrament, and has put no obstacle (*obex*) such as mortal sin in its way. In such an instance, the recipient would be said to have received, not the sacrament itself, but the *res sacramenti*, the ultimate reality or effect of the sacrament, which is grace. A valid sacrament is not necessarily a fruitful sacrament, and an invalid sacrament is not necessarily unfruitful. St. Thomas Aquinas (1225-74) reasoned that God can bestow the effects of the sacraments without the sacraments themselves, imparting grace and sanctification in other ways.[8] This view would later receive official approbation by the Church, particularly with regard to the sacraments of Baptism and Penance.[9]

It would be difficult to overlook the significance of these developments. Augustine's sacramental theology made it possible for the Catholic Church to recognize the "validity," the objective reality, of sacraments administered outside the Church's visible unity. Ordinations performed by schismatic bishops are true ordinations, and the sacramental powers that come with Order are passed on, albeit without the Church's approbation. As for schismatic congregations without bishops, their sacraments (with the exception of Baptism) are simply invalid. However, Scholastic sacramental theology made it possible to admit that schismatic sacraments, whether invalid or simply illicit, might even be received fruitfully, provided the recipient sincerely desire the sacramental grace. This should be kept in mind when discussing ministry and sacraments beyond the visible and verifiable apostolic succession.

---

[8] *Summa Theol.*, III, q. 64, ad 7c.
[9] Council of Trent, Sess. VI, *Decretum de iustificatione*, cap. 4, 14; DS 1524, 1543. Cf. CCC 1257.

*4.2. Medieval thought on the sacrament of Order*

The Council of Florence (1439-42) produced a detailed exposition of the doctrine of the sacraments. Especially relevant to our study of the apostolic succession is the Council's *Decree for the Armenians* (1439), which followed closely St. Thomas' brief treatise *On the articles of faith and the sacraments of the Church*. After enumerating the seven sacraments and their effects, the Decree stated:

> All these sacraments are brought to completion by three components: by things as *matter*, by words as *form*, and by the person of the minister effecting the sacrament with the *intention* of doing what the Church does. And if any one of these three is lacking, the sacrament is not effected. Among these sacraments, there are three, Baptism, Confirmation and Holy Orders, which print on the soul an indelible character, that is, a certain spiritual sign distinguishing the recipient from others. Hence, these are not given more than once to one person. The other four do not imprint this character and may be repeated.[10]

Thereafter follows a treatment of each of the sacraments. On the sacrament of Order, the Decree reflected the prevailing opinion of its time concerning the crucial sacramental gesture or "matter":

> The sixth sacrament is Holy Orders. Its matter is that which is handed over in the conferring of the order: the priesthood, for example, is conferred by the presentation of the chalice containing the wine and the paten holding the bread; the diaconate by the giving of the book of the Gospels; the subdiaconate by the handing-over of an empty chalice covered with an empty paten.... The form of the order of priesthood is this: "Receive the power of offering sacrifice in the

---

[10] DS 1312-13/TCT 663; emphasis added.

> Church for the living and the dead in the name of the Father and of the Son and of the Holy Spirit." ...The ordinary minister of this sacrament is the bishop. The effect of the sacrament is an increase of grace so that one may be a suitable minister.[11]

The Decree is pertinent to our study for a couple of reasons. One reason concerns its affirmation that there is no valid sacrament if *matter*, *form*, or an authorized minister with proper *intention* is lacking. And where there is no sacrament of Order, there is no apostolic succession. This will be the central ecumenical issue with regard to Protestantism and Anglicanism, about which more will be said later.

Another reason for the Decree's significance concerns the episcopate specifically. Conspicuously absent is mention of the consecration of a bishop. From the fourth century onward there was a tendency to regard the episcopate and the presbyterate as theologically equal. Owing chiefly to the great emphasis they placed on the spiritual powers (*potestas*) of Church officeholders, most medieval theologians did not consider the episcopate a grade of Order separate from the presbyterate. The episcopacy as a sacrament is not mentioned in the Decree. The bishop is simply recognized as the ordinary minister of the sacrament of Order.

For St. Thomas and his contemporaries, the Eucharist is the center and uniting principle for the sacrament of Order.[12] As St. Bonaventure put it succinctly: *ordo est ad sacrificium administrandum*, "Order is for the ministering of sacrifice."[13] Because a bishop possesses no powers with respect to the Eucharist which a presbyter

---

[11] DS 1326/TCT 839.

[12] For instance, *Summa Theol.*, III, q. 82, a. 1; *Suppl.*, q. 37, a. 2. Vatican II upheld the validity of this theology of Order for our own time in PO 2: "The ministry of priests is directed to [the Eucharistic sacrifice] and finds its consummation in it"; cf. PO 5.

[13] *In quartum librum Sententiarum*, dist. 24, pars 1, a. 2, q. 3.

does not already have, the Scholastics reasoned that the special character of the episcopate relates to jurisdiction and administration. Thus with regard to priests, one spoke of a power over the Body of Christ in the Eucharist (*potestas in corpus eucharisticum*), and with regard to bishops of a power over the Mystical Body, the Church (*potestas in corpus mysticum*).[14] St. Thomas could admit, however, that in some sense the episcopate is sacramental because of its role of headship (*principalitas*) over the Mystical Body.[15] The relationship between the power of Order and the power of jurisdiction, especially as they relate to the episcopal office, would remain unclear until the Second Vatican Council.

Finally, the Decree is noteworthy because of what it says about the "matter" or external sign of the sacrament of Order. It recognizes the *traditio instrumentorum*, the handing-over of the sacred vessels used in the Eucharistic sacrifice, not the more ancient laying-on of hands, as the matter of the sacrament. (It should be noted, however, that the Council upheld the validity of the Greek Church's ordination rite, which did not include the *traditio instrumentorum*). In the Middle Ages this rite was observed throughout the Western Church, and was thought by many theologians to be necessary for sacramental validity. Like the debate on the sacramentality of the episcopate, the controversy over the essential matter of Order would remain unsettled until the middle of the twentieth century.

## 4.3. Reformation and Counter-Reformation ecclesiology in brief

Ecclesiology made its entrance as a theological system only in the twentieth century. In the Middle Ages, it had no place in the systematized theology then evolving. The juridical and insti-

---

[14] Vorgrimler, 254.
[15] Nichols, 80.

tutional demands made on the Church excluded any ecclesiology and produced rather a canonical exposition of the Church. The Church's inner nature was not its object, but rather her institutional aspect and social power, especially with regard to the struggles between Church and State.

The medieval divines composed no independent tracts or *summæ* of ecclesiology *per se*. In point of fact, the reality of the Church so spontaneously and totally penetrated the life of the Fathers and Scholastic theologians that no room remained for any direct theological reflection on the Church herself. This is especially more true of the Fathers than the Scholastics. At the end of the Middle Ages a new tendency gradually appeared in apologetics against the Waldensians, Lollards and Hussites.

The Protestant Reformation in the sixteenth century made a strong demand for answers to many questions. However one might wish to criticize their doctrine and tactics, the Reformers awakened the Church to such vital truths as the primacy of grace, the priesthood of all the baptized, the centrality of Scripture and the preaching of it, and Church office as service. One Lutheran theologian sums up the position of Luther and the other Reformers in the following terms:

> When they stressed the importance of faith, of justification by grace alone, of the priesthood of the faithful, they thought of themselves not as innovators but as men who stood on scriptural and apostolic ground. So convinced were they of the biblical and apostolic character of the message they proclaimed that they could not renounce it even at the insistence of the religious authorities whom they respected so highly.[16]

---

[16] Warren A. Quanbeck, "A Contemporary View of Apostolic Succession," in *Lutherans and Catholics in Dialogue*, Vol. 4, *Eucharist and Ministry* (Washington: United States Catholic Conference, 1970), 178-88, at 179.

The Reformers affirmed these principles with a view to restoring the Church by bringing her back to her own sources. What Church authorities opposed were not these principles themselves — they are indeed scriptural and apostolic — but rather the conclusions which the Reformers began to draw from them, conclusions opposed to Scripture itself and to the whole of Tradition. Certain aspects of the New Testament were over-emphasized and others neglected.

Martin Luther's (1483-1546) stress on "alone" led to exaggerations in almost every sphere (Scripture *alone*, grace *alone*, faith *alone*), so that it was soon as open to misunderstanding as the Catholic "and" (Scripture *and* Tradition, grace *and* free will, faith *and* good works).[17] The entire Church was to be judged by his criterion of justification by faith alone. If it is faith alone that reconciles the sinner with God, then the Church's sacraments can only be external signs of the grace or salvation received through faith in Christ's atoning sacrifice. Whatever smacked of Galatian legalism or salvation by external deeds (what Protestants pejoratively call

---

[17] Küng, *The Church*, 280. Following is a similar assessment, from a semantic perspective, by Cecily Hastings, untitled essay in *Born Catholics*, assembled by P.J. Sheed (New York: Sheed & Ward, 1954), 170:

> As to the alternatives provided by divisions amongst Christians: the points of disagreement between various forms of Christian opinion and the Catholic Church are, for me, decided by the fact that each such divergence has to be expressed, sooner or later, by the word "merely." I mean that whenever there is a choice between giving to some part of the Christian revelation either a more expansive, many-dimensioned, richly complex, open interpretation or, alternatively, a narrower, flatter, thinner, more restricted one, the former is always the Catholic one. The points of departure, all along the road from Unitarianism upwards, are marked by some rejection of the Catholic meaning whose expression involves a "merely." "When He said 'I and the Father are one,' He *merely* meant..."; "The rite of baptism is *merely*..."; "What He did at the Last Supper was *merely*..."; "'I will give to thee the keys of the kingdom of heaven' *merely* means..." and so on and so on. And, as far as I am concerned, any sentence with "merely" in it, applied to divine revelation, is condemned by the presence of the word. Whatever else God's word to man might be, it would not be "merely" anything.

"works-righteousness") was repudiated as unevangelical. Certain tendencies toward Pelagian errors or superstition, at least in popular piety, provoked Luther to reject the sacrifice of the Mass as a futile (at best) and blasphemous (at worst) effort to earn grace and salvation.[18]

Luther and the other Reformers drew over-hasty conclusions also regarding the priesthood of all the faithful and the ordained priesthood. By Baptism received in faith, all believers are consecrated as priests (1 P 2:5, 9-10). Of course, this biblical doctrine does not exclude a ministerial priesthood. But in his treatise *On the Babylonian Captivity of the Church* (1520), Luther denied that Order was a sacrament supported by Scripture, and insisted that ordination was merely an ecclesiastical ceremony. The ordained or ministerial priesthood, in the Protestant view, arises from delegation by the royal priesthood of the baptized. All the baptized have the same powers with respect to word and sacraments, but no one is to use this power without the consent of the congregation.

> However, Lutheranism early became much less radical on this issue, in part by way of reaction to still more heterodox groups springing up to its left. Thus, Melanchthon, in his *Loci communes*, declared himself willing to count Order as a sacrament so long as its ministry of word and sacrament was not taken to include the offering of sacrifice for the living

---

[18] See e.g., *The Smalcald Articles* (1537) 2.2. A good synopsis of the Lutheran understanding of the Mass is that of Liam G. Walsh, O.P., "Eucharist: the word," chap. in *The Sacraments of Initiation*, Geoffrey Chapman Theology Library Series, gen. ed. Michael Richards, no. 7 (London: Cassell Publishers Ltd., 1988), 246:

> The real business of the Sacrament [of the Eucharist] is the giving of the grace of God, in the face of which humans have nothing to offer but acceptance of justification in faith and repentance.... Ministers of the Euchanst did not make a sacrifice.... The Reformers did affirm strongly that the Supper is a memorial of the sacrifice of Christ. But it is a remembering of the sacrifice of Christ, not as something that is being offered but as something from which the fruits of salvation are now being drawn. The movement from the divine (in Christ) to the human (in sinners) is recognized but not the movement from humans, caught up in the human sacrifice of Christ, to the divine (in the Father).

and the dead (for this was a view of the Eucharist remark-
ably resistant to combination with the Lutheran "by faith
alone"). In his *Defence of the Augsburg Confession*,
Melanchthon, though uncompromising on this point, regards the inherited ministerial Order as rendered venerable
by long-standing custom, and to be preserved on grounds
of the public good of the Church. Only the non-coopera-
tion of the Catholic episcopate with the Reform prevents
the latter's supporters from keeping that Order whole and
entire.[19]

Taking up the ideas of the Bohemian Jan Hus (ca. 1369-1415)
and the Englishman John Wyclif (ca. 1329-84), who are sometimes
called the "proto-Protestants," the French Reformer Jean Calvin
(1509-64) and others to the "left" of Luther and Melanchthon conceived of the Church as essentially a congregation of Christian
believers predestined to eternal life, not to be identified with the
institutional Church, since its members are known only to God.[20]
The Church, then, is essentially invisible, though Christians need
the pastoral office for preaching and discipline. The authority of
the Christian ministry was vague and uncertain, and ecclesiastical
polity varied from place to place.

On the Continent, simple priests (presbyters) were used to
ordain new clergy. Neither "papist" nor "reformed" would necessarily have thought these ordinations ineffectual on the grounds of
the minister alone, given the general assumption at the time that
the presbyterate was the essential Order of the ministry. It might
be inexpedient that a presbyter should ordain, but there was no
theological objection. Nor were such ordinations unprecedented.[21]

---

[19] Nichols, 91-92.

[20] Calvin, for example, defined the Church as "the company of the faithful whom God
has elected and elected to eternal life" (Catechism of the Church of Geneva).

[21] Pope Boniface IX's Bull *Sacræ Religionis* of 1400 (DS 1145) conceded to the Abbot of
the monastery of St. Osith in Essex, who was not a bishop, and to his successors, the

Consequently, in most of the areas which went over to Protestant-ism, the apostolic succession of bishops came to an end.[22] In its place, an "apostolicity of the spirit" was emphasized.

Having broken from the papal Church, the Reformation Churches laid great stress on apostolic teaching and *praxis* over against inherited office. A Church belongs to the apostolic succession as long as it proclaims the Gospel and lives according to it (cf. 1 Cor 9:14). As one French Reformed Church pastor explains:

> I do not think it would be contradicting the deepest intention of the Reformers to say that in reforming the Church they wanted to recover the true apostolic succession, which in their eyes did not mean simply a legal pedigree but rather the faithful exercise of the ministry entrusted by Christ to the apostles.[23]

From the Catholic side, Swiss theologian Hans Küng offers a similar evaluation:

> They were convinced that they had to choose between a succession which would perpetuate the apostolic spirit, life, and activity and the succession to the apostolic office. It cannot be denied that the succession in office of those bishops who were little concerned with the apostolic office, the apostolic life and activity, had in fact to a large extent been voided of its original significance and had therefore become formalized indeed. The Reformers broke away from the

---

power to confer minor and major Orders, including the priesthood, on the members of their community. (Because of the objection of Bishop Robert of London, who had the right of patronage in the monastery, this privilege was revoked three years later by the Bull *Apostolicæ Sedis* of the same Pope [DS 1146].) Pope Martin V's Bull *Gerentes ad vos* of 1427 (DS 1290) granted a similar privilege, for a five-year period, to the Abbot of the Cistercian monastery at Altzelle in Upper Saxony.

[22] An exception would be the Lutheran Churches in Scandinavia.

[23] Jean-Jacques von Allmen, "Ordination — A Sacrament? A Protestant Reply," *Concilium*, vol. 74, *The Plurality of Ministries* [henceforth *Concilium* 74], ed. Hans Küng and Walter Kasper (New York: Herder & Herder, 1972), 40-48, at 43.

episcopal succession only under compulsion, and the separation was regarded as an emergency solution by the Reformers throughout their lives.[24]

In response to the Reformers, an eminently apologetic
ecclesiology emerged which stressed the juridical and hierarchical
aspects of the Church, but without resorting to a purely visible
Church.[25] Her spiritual or internal dimension took second place.
The towering figure of the Counter-Reformation, the Jesuit Cardinal Robert Bellarmine (1542-1621), insisted that the Church is
a reality as visible as the Kingdom of France, or the Republic of
Venice. The visible Church of Christ is to be identified by the presence of three bonds existing among her members: first, the profession of the same faith (*vinculum symbolicum*); second, the sharing
of the same sacraments (*vinculum sacramentale*); and third, legitimate pastors in union with the successor of the Apostle Peter (*vinculum hierarchicum*).[26]

Like Irenaeus and the other Church Fathers long before,
Catholic apologists from Trent until modern times stressed the
uninterrupted sequence of ordinations going back to the apostles.
An Oxford sermon of Msgr. Ronald Knox (1888-1957), who as
an Anglican followed the path to Rome marked out three-quar-
ters of a century earlier by John Henry Newman (1801-90), exem-
plifies the Catholic apologetics of the post-Tridentine period:

> In the New Testament, it is not enough to be called; you
> must be sent; St. Paul himself, a called man if ever there
> was one, was sent by the Church at Antioch when he be-
> gan his travels. And that sending has been going on con-

---

[24] Hans Küng, *Structures of the Church*, trans. Salvator Attanasio (New York: Thomas Nelson & Sons, 1964), 183.

[25] Cf. *Catech. Trid.* 1.10.21: Insofar as the Church is recognizable *fide solum*, "only by faith," she is hidden and invisible.

[26] St. Robert Bellarmine, *De controversiis*, II, lib. 3, *De Ecclesia militante*, cap. 2; ed. J. Giuliano (Naples, 1957), 2:75.

tinuously through the ages; the Church has always had her own hierarchy of commissioned officials, following one another in unbroken succession. The other denominations may claim that their ministers are called; but who sent them? Always, if you examine their line of succession, there is a flaw in the title-deeds; a human agent has stepped in and interrupted, by his interference, the unbroken succession of *sent men* to whom our Lord made His promises.[27]

So, too, the impressive rhetoric of Cardinal James Gibbons (1834-1921), the most influential American prelate at the turn of the nineteenth and twentieth centuries:

> The Catholic Church can easily vindicate the title of Apostolic, because she derives her origin from the apostles. Every priest and bishop can trace his genealogy to the first disciples of Christ with as much facility as the most remote branch of a vine can be traced to the main stem.
> All the Catholic clergy in the United States, for instance, were ordained only by Bishops who are in active communion with the See of Rome. These bishops themselves received their commissions from the Bishop of Rome.... Like the Evangelist Luke, who traces the genealogy of our Savior back to Adam and to God, we can trace the pedigree of Pius IX to Peter and to Christ. There is not a link wanting in the chain which binds the humblest priest in the land to the Prince of the Apostles....
> Count over the bishops from the very See of St. Peter, and mark, in the list of Fathers, how one succeeded the other. This is the rock against which the proud gates of hell do not prevail.[28]

While these two examples focus too exclusively on lineage to be altogether satisfactory accounts of the apostolic succession, they

---

[27] *University & Anglican Sermons of Ronald A. Knox*, ed. Philip Caraman, S.J. (New York: Sheed & Ward, 1963), 236.

[28] James Cardinal Gibbons, *The Faith of Our Fathers*, rev. ed. (New York: P.J. Kenedy & Sons, 1917), 48-49.

do represent an important testimony to the visible, tangible dimension of the apostolic succession, which was highly esteemed from apostolic times. It is time now to examine the official doctrine of the Catholic Church, from the Reformation to the present, with regard to those matters relating to the apostolic succession.

Chapter Five

# Dogmatic Pronouncements
# on Apostolic Succession

Thus far we have seen that, from earliest times, the apostolic succession has been an essential element in the Church's self-understanding. Scripture and the early Church Fathers and apologists bear witness to the fact that bishops are the rightful inheritors of the apostolic ministry and guardians of true doctrine. Beginning with the Council of Trent (1545-63), the apostolic succession is no longer simply the form of Tradition, but an integral part of Tradition itself: the apostolic succession is explicitly "dogmatized," as it were. Whereas the First Vatican Council (1869-70) simply reiterated Trent's teaching that bishops are successors of the apostles, the Second Vatican Council (1962-65) worked out a theology of the episcopate, and explained *how* bishops succeed the apostles. It is now time to consider the apostolic succession specifically as a defined doctrine of the Catholic Church, turning our attention to these three most recent general Councils.

## 5.1. Trent

Against the teaching of the Reformers, Trent asserted that the ecclesiastical ministry is not based on the universal priesthood of the baptized and does not derive from it; nor do all Christians

59

share the same spiritual power equally and indiscriminately (*promiscue*). In the Church there are diverse charisms and functions, in accordance with apostolic Church order. Ordination is truly a sacrament with solid biblical foundation:

> Since it is very clear from the testimony of Sacred Scrip-
> ture, from apostolic Tradition, and from the unanimous
> agreement of the Fathers, that grace is conferred through
> holy ordination, which is effected by words and external
> signs, no one should doubt that Orders is truly and prop-
> erly one of the seven sacraments of holy Church. For the
> Apostle says: "I admonish thee to stir up the grace of God
> which is in thee by the laying-on of my hands. For God has
> not given us the spirit of fear, but of power and of love and
> of prudence" [2 Tm 1:6-7; cf. 1 Tm 4:14].[1]

Furthermore, the Council declared that the bishops are the successors of the apostles and belong in a "special way" to the hierarchy of the Church:

> Therefore the holy Council declares that, besides the other
> ecclesiastical grades, the bishops, who have succeeded the
> apostles, belong in a special way to the hierarchical order;[2]

While leaving open the question whether the episcopate is a
sacrament, the Council taught that bishops exercise certain sacramental functions that simple priests cannot perform. By virtue of
the superiority of their grade, the bishops are the proper and ordinary ministers of the sacraments of Order and Confirmation:

> … and "placed" (as the Apostle says) "by the Holy Spirit to
> rule the Church of God" [Ac 20:28], they are superior to
> priests [*presbyteris*], and can confer the sacrament of Con-

---

[1] Council of Trent, Sess. XXIII, *Doctrina de sacramento ordinis*, cap. 3; DS 1766/TCT 842.
[2] *Ibid.*, cap. 4; DS 1768/TCT 843.

firmation, can ordain ministers for the Church, and they have the power to perform many other functions that those of an inferior grade cannot.[3]

Trent's only criticism of pastors who had not been ordained by "canonical and ecclesiastical power" was that they were not "legitimate" ministers of word and sacrament. Such ministries are not declared to be null and void, but simply illegitimate:

> If anyone says… that those who have not been rightly ordained by ecclesiastical and canonical power and have not been sent, but come from some other source, are lawful ministers of the word and of the sacraments: let him be *anathema*.[4]

Those who usurp the ecclesiastical ministries on their own authority are not to be recognized as legitimate ministers of the Church ("*omnes non Ecclesiæ ministros*"), but — with a reference to John 10:1 — as thieves and robbers who have not entered through the gate.[5] "The 'gate' is, evidently, the apostolic succession, whereby the original apostolic mandate is continued sacramentally over time."[6]

## 5.2. Vatican I

The outbreak of the Franco-Prussian War in the summer of 1870, and the end of papal temporal control over Rome, forced the First Vatican Council to an abrupt end without finishing the work it had planned. The Council Fathers did not have sufficient time

---

[3] *Ibid.*

[4] Council of Trent, Sess. XXIII, *Canones de sacramento ordinis*, can. 7; DS 1777/TCT 850.

[5] Council of Trent, Sess. XXIII, *Doctrina de sacramento ordinis*, cap. 4; DS 1769/TCT 843.

[6] Nichols, 100.

to work out a theology of the episcopate. They simply restated the position of Trent, without further elaboration: "The bishops have been placed by the Holy Spirit [Ac 20:28] as successors of the apostles."[7] We must wait until the Second Vatican Council, almost a century later, for the resolution of certain questions concerning the episcopate.

### 5.3. Vatican II

The Second Vatican Council had a great deal to say about the office of bishops. It is said that Pope Paul VI considered the theology of the episcopate to be the most important question the Council took up. The "Dogmatic Constitution on the Church," *Lumen Gentium*, reiterates the teaching of the Councils of Trent and Vatican I:

> The bishops have by divine institution taken the place of the apostles as pastors of the Church, in such wise that whoever listens to them is listening to Christ and whoever despises them despises Christ and Him Who sent Christ (cf. Lk 10:16).[8]

The same article of *Lumen Gentium* prefaces this reaffirmation by explaining how the bishops have taken the place of the apostles:

> In order that the mission entrusted to them [= the apostles] might be continued after their death, they consigned, by will and testament, as it were, to their immediate collaborators the duty of completing and consolidating the work they had

---

[7] Vatican Council I, Sess. IV, Dogmatic Const. I *De Ecclesia Christi* (=*Pastor Æternus*), cap. 3; DS 3061.

[8] LG 20; cf. CD 2.

begun, urging them to tend to the whole flock, in which the Holy Spirit had appointed them to shepherd the Church of God (cf. Ac 20:28). They accordingly designated such men and then made the ruling that likewise on their death other proven men should take over their ministry. Amongst those various offices which have been exercised in the Church from the earliest times the chief place, according to the witness of Tradition, is held by the function of those who, through their appointment to the dignity and responsibility of bishop, and in virtue consequently of the unbroken succession, going back to the beginning, are regarded as transmitters of the apostolic line. Thus, according to the testimony of St. Irenaeus, the apostolic Tradition is manifested and preserved in the whole world by those who were made bishops by the apostles and by their successors down to our own time.

Thereafter *Lumen Gentium* pronounces on a matter which was left unresolved by the Councils of Trent and Vatican I:

The fullness of the sacrament of Orders is conferred by episcopal consecration, that fullness, namely, which both in the liturgical tradition of the Church and in the language of the Fathers of the Church is called the high priesthood, the acme of the sacred ministry.[9]

With this declaration, Vatican II settled a disagreement in Catholic theology reaching back to the fourth century. In the previous chapter we saw that the medieval distinction between sacrament and jurisdiction led many theologians to regard episcopal consecration as non-sacramental. The presbyter, not the bishop, was looked upon as having the fullness of priesthood. Now the Council Fathers opted to endorse the more ancient view.

The episcopate is the fullness of the sacrament of Order, and

---

[9] LG 21.

not merely an office or dignity above the presbyterate. Moreover, Vatican II joins the power of Order and the power of jurisdiction. Because the episcopate is the high priesthood, consecration confers the threefold *munus* of sanctifying, teaching and governing, corresponding to Christ's own threefold office as Priest, Prophet and King.[10] The Council deliberately chose to speak of the bishop's *munus* rather than his *potestas*, his power, in order to show that the episcopate is not just a matter of jurisdiction. Power is ordered to action (*in actu expedita*) and is not given without delegation from the Pope, whereas the threefold office comes immediately from Christ through episcopal consecration.[11] Not only the Bishop of Rome but indeed every bishop is rightly looked upon as the vicar of Christ.[12]

By their consecration, the bishops enter into the apostolic succession, which has a collegial character.

> The order of bishops is the successor to the college of the apostles in their role as teachers and pastors, and in it the apostolic college is perpetuated.[13]

The bishop exercises his pastoral office authentically only in union with the Pope. "Together with their head, the Supreme Pontiff, and never apart from him," the bishops exercise "supreme and full authority over the universal Church."[14]

It is in this frame of mind that we will enter, in the following chapter, the contemporary theological discussion of the apostolic succession, with its ecumenical priorities. Before going into this,

---

[10] LG 19.

[11] Cf. "Nota explicativa prævia," in *Acta Synodalia Sacrosancti Concilii Oecumenici Vaticani Secundi* 3.8 (Vatican City, 1976), 11.

[12] LG 21.

[13] LG 22.

[14] LG 22.

however, it may be worthwhile to digress just briefly enough to take notice of another matter which Trent and Vatican I did not address. The matter pertains to the apostolic succession insofar as it concerns the sacrament of Order specifically.

Vatican II thought it worth mentioning that entrance into the apostolic ministry comes through ordination by prayer and the ancient gesture of the laying-on of hands:

> In fact, from Tradition, which is expressed especially in the liturgical rites and in the customs of both the Eastern and Western Church, it is abundantly clear that by the imposition of hands and through the words of the consecration, the grace of the Holy Spirit is given, and a sacred character is impressed in such wise that bishops, in a resplendent and visible manner, take the place of Christ Himself, Teacher, Shepherd and Priest, and act as His representatives (*in eius persona*).[15]

Here the Council reaffirmed what Pope Pius XII had decreed two decades earlier regarding the rite of ordination, namely: the practice of the ancient Church is to be considered normative. For centuries theologians debated whether the sign of the sacrament of Order, its "matter," was the laying-on of hands, the handing-over of the paten with the bread and of the chalice with the wine, or both. Without giving decisions on the speculative questions involved, Pius XII's Apostolic Constitution *Sacramentum Ordinis* of 1947 settled the controversy by stating that the proper sacramental sign or "matter" of ordination is the laying-on of hands, nothing else. The supplanting of the more traditional form by the presentation of the sacred vessels was suppressed.[16]

---

[15] LG 21. Citing this article, CCC 1575 reads: "Thus, it is Christ whose gift it is that some be apostles, others pastors. He continues to act through the bishops."

[16] DS 3857-61.

Cardinal Ratzinger finds Pius XII's decision ecclesiologically significant for a couple of reasons. By recognizing "the problem of peculiarly medieval developments," the form for the sacrament of Order in the Latin Rite "was explicitly changed to conform with the standard of the universal Church." The practice of the early Church "was specifically acknowledged as normative" not only for the Eastern Church but also the Western Church.

Taking into account the intimate union of theology and ritual, the ecclesiological significance of Pius XII's decision runs much deeper than these "cosmetic" changes might suggest. By favoring the more ancient form, the Latin Church reclaimed the pneumatological (and not simply the Christological) orientation of the sacrament of Order.[17] The imposition of hands is the traditional expression of the conferral of the Holy Spirit; whereas, by contrast, the medieval rite was formed on the pattern of investiture in a secular office. Eastern Christians have often faulted Roman Catholicism for paying insufficient attention to the work of the Holy Spirit in the life of the Church. As one Greek Orthodox bishop comments: "Because the role of the Spirit has been neglected in the West, the Church has come to be regarded too much as an institution of this world, governed in terms of earthly power and jurisdiction."[18] The Latin Church's return to the older and more pneumatologically illustrative rite was another step toward bridging the divide between Eastern and Western Christianity.

We move on now to consider what theologians have been saying about the apostolic succession in the period following the Second Vatican Council.

---

[17] PCT, 240 ff. On pneumatological import, cf. Osborne, 328-30.
[18] Bishop Kallistos (Timothy) Ware, *The Orthodox Church*, rev. ed. (New York: Viking Penguin Inc., 1983), 223.

Chapter Six

# Contemporary Thought
# on the Apostolic Succession

One of the difficult tasks of theology is to preserve the inner equi-
librium of revealed truth in an organic unity of tensions.[1] Theologians are aware of the pitfalls that come with overemphasizing one
constitutive dimension of the apostolic succession while neglect-
ing the others. The legitimacy of episcopal succession cannot be
severed from the continuity in Christian faith and life. The episcopal office is no isolated reality, but finds its authenticity only in
relation to Tradition. It is time now to consider in what sense the
bishops of the Catholic Church are the legitimate successors of the
apostles.

---

[1] This is the genius of Catholicism, observes Karl Adam: "It could be shown in detail how
Catholicism has sometimes repelled and rejected outright an heretical position with all
its implications, reasons and consequences in order to prevent any contamination of
revealed truth, and then, when the danger of such contamination was past, has taken
over those elements of truth which heresy had grasped but wrongly emphasized, and
moulding them into harmony with the whole of revelation, has consciously built them
into her teaching and maintained them." — *The Spirit of Catholicism*, rev. ed., trans.
Justin McCann (Garden City, N.Y.: Doubleday Image Books, 1954), 158-59. Also see
Msgr. Charles Journet, *The Wisdom of Faith: An Introduction to Theology*, trans. R.F.
Smith, S.J. (Westminster, Md.: The Newman Press, 1952), 22-23, with a reference to
St. Thomas Aquinas, *Summa Theologiae*, II-II, q. 1, a. 2.

*6.1. The bishops' relationship to the apostles*

Concerning the relationship of the apostles to Christ, "the apostles do not replace the only foundation, but their *communio* with Christ, the foundation, is itself in turn fundamental for the Church."[2] Just as the apostles were the first witnesses to Christ, so the bishops are witnesses to the apostles.[3] A bishop stands in historical succession to the apostles only by preserving communion with his fellow bishops and never in isolation from them. As Jesuit theologian Fr. Karl Rahner explains:

> The episcopal college is regarded in the whole Christian Tradition as the successor to the apostolic college. That the bishops are the successors of the apostles in their [inheritable] office is Catholic dogma. If an episcopal college existed, then — assuming this teaching of the Faith — it can and must be said that the episcopal *college* as such is the successor of the apostolic *college*, as such.[4]

The principle of "corporate succession" is reflected in a 1985 Catechism authored largely by Bishop Kasper under the aegis of the German Bishops' Conference:

> We should not misunderstand the doctrine of apostolic succession. It does not mean that the bishops are new apostles. The office of the apostles is unique, but some particular apostolic functions must, according to the words of Jesus Christ, be continued beyond the time of the apostles. So we must *distinguish between the unique office of the apostles and the permanent apostolic office*. The bishops are successors of

---

[2] Karl Rahner, S.J., ed., *Encyclopedia of Theology. The Concise Sacramentum Mundi* (New York: The Seabury Press, 1975), s.v. "Apostolic Succession," by Wilhelm Breuning.

[3] Antonio Javierre, S.D.B., *Apostolic Succession: Rethinking a Barrier to Christian Unity* (Glen Rock, N.J.: Paulist Press, 1968), 25.

[4] Karl Rahner, S.J., *Bishops: Their Status and Function* (Baltimore: Helicon Press, 1964), 19.

the apostles only in the second sense. This succession should not be misunderstood in a purely external way, as if it were merely a chain of the imposition of hands or an uninterrupted occupation of the episcopal sees. It needs to be seen *in the total context.*[5]

In the same vein, Ehrhardt admonishes:

> What cannot be proved is that any of the Twelve instituted a particular succession of bishops, or that the particular ministerial succession which, according to the Pastoral Epistles, was instituted by St. Paul has been followed down to our time. As a matter of fact, it is significant for our own argument that, although the Pastoral Epistles contemplated such a succession, the tradition of the Catholic Church contains no reference to any line of bishops in the succession of St. Paul.[6]

According to Miller, the apostles are distinguished from their episcopal successors in four respects:

> *First*, bishops are not eyewitnesses to revelation, as the Twelve were; instead, they are ministerial heads of communities who give authoritative testimony to the deposit of faith which has already been formed. Only the original apostles are the Church's irreplaceable foundation (cf. Eph 2:20), the foundation of the new Jerusalem (cf. Rv 21:14). *Second*, because of the Spirit's unique presence in the apostolic Church, the apostles' teaching itself constituted the deposit of faith which later generations were to preserve. Unlike the apostles, bishops are not themselves vessels of revelation. *Third*, the apostles individually enjoyed the charism of

---

[5] German Bishops' Conference, *The Church's Confession of Faith: A Catholic Catechism for Adults*, ed. Mark Jordan, trans. Stephen Wentworth Arndt (San Francisco: Ignatius Press, 1989), 239, italics in original. (First published in German as *Katholischer Erwachsenen Katechismus: Das Glaubensbekenntnis der Kirche* [Bonn: Verband der Diözesen Deutschlands, 1985].)

[6] Ehrhardt, *The Apostolic Succession*, 21.

preaching the Gospel without error. Bishops, however, possess this charism only as a collegial body. *Lastly*, except for the Pope, no bishop succeeds to a particular apostle, though he might succeed to an apostolic see. Instead, each bishop is accepted as a member of the episcopal college which succeeds as a body to the apostolic college.[7]

Synthesizing these views, we find that theologians acknowledge a tangible apostolic succession, but do not view it primarily as something passed individually from one bishop to another. Rather, the apostolic succession is connected with the succession of the entire college of bishops, which continues the college of the apostles. The apostolic succession is not individual, but "catholic": the college of bishops in its entirety stands in direct succession to the college of apostles and carries on their mission.

*6.2. The effects of Vatican II's ecclesiology on the doctrine of apostolic succession*

With the Second Vatican Council's renewed ecclesiology a new problem arose. As the Council teaches, the apostolic succession exists within the episcopal college, which is headed by the Roman Pontiff.[8] Yet the same Council affirms of the separated Eastern Churches that

> these Churches, although separated from us, yet possess true sacraments, above all — by apostolic succession — the priesthood and the Eucharist, whereby they are still joined to us in closest intimacy.[9]

---

[7] Miller, *The Shepherd and the Rock*, 58.

[8] LG 22; CD 4.

[9] UR 15. Vatican II spoke of the separated Eastern Churches without mentioning the Orthodox Church by name. The reason is that the Council Fathers also had in mind the Eastern Churches which are not in canonical communion with the Ecumenical Patriarch of Constantinople, but which nonetheless are within the apostolic succession.

Despite the fact that they have broken communion with the Roman Pontiff, these Churches remain within the apostolic succession. To this will naturally come the reply: but if the apostolic succession exists only in the universal episcopate whose head is the Pope, how can the Catholic Church acknowledge a real succession of apostolic ministry, and hence the validity of Order and sacraments, outside her communion? It would seem that the Council has contradicted itself on this matter.

One attempt to explain how a Church not in communion with the head of the episcopal college can nonetheless possess the apostolic succession employs the philosophical categories of "matter" and "form." Rahner and Vorgrimler explain that the bishops of the separated Eastern Churches are, "by reason of valid episcopal consecration, *materially but not formally*, true successors of the apostles."[10] They define the apostolic succession as "the legitimation of office and authority by their valid derivation from the twelve apostles, who received this office and authority directly from Christ."

According to this definition, the apostolic succession is viewed

---

These Churches, which severed communion with the rest of the Christian world following the Councils of Ephesus (431) and Chalcedon (451), are collectively known by various titles: the non-Chalcedonian Churches, the Oriental Orthodox Churches, or the Ancient Churches of the East. They are: the Assyrian Oriental Church (formerly called Nestorian), the Armenian Apostolic Church, the Coptic Church, the Ethiopian Church, the Syro-Jacobite Church and the Syrian Church in India. At various times over the centuries, segments of the faithful of each of these Churches restored communion with Rome. Today, they constitute, respectively, the Chaldean (Syro-Malabar, in India), Armenian, Coptic, Ethiopian, Syrian and Syro-Malankar Catholic Churches.

Similarly, Vatican II did not use the term "Protestant" in reference to the separated Western communities, perhaps because not all of these denominations issue from the Reformation or espouse the doctrines of classical Protestantism (e.g., the Old Catholic Church, the Christian Science Church, the Seventh-day Adventist Church, and assorted Pentecostal bodies).

[10] Karl Rahner, S.J., and Herbert Vorgrimler, *Theological Dictionary*, ed. Cornelius Ernst, O.P., trans. Richard Strachan (New York: Herder & Herder, 1965), s.v. "Apostolic Succession"; emphasis added.

under two aspects: one *material* (pertaining to office), the other *formal* (pertaining to authority or jurisdiction). "Material succession," which confers the power of Order, is given as "sacramental consecration by validly consecrated bishops" who stand within the apostolic succession; "formal succession," which confers the power of jurisdiction, is given as "the office-bearer's full communion with and subordination to the Church, and thus to its supreme office-bearer, the Pope, the legitimate successor of the head of the apostolic college." Hence the Orthodox Churches belong to the apostolic succession materially but not formally. The same holds for the so-called non-Chalcedonian Eastern Churches and, in the West, the Churches of the Old Catholic communion. As we noted in the previous chapter, Vatican II taught that episcopal consecration brings immediately with it the threefold office, including that of governance (*episkopē*); yet the empowerment to exercise this office (as of the others) requires additionally the authorization of the head of the episcopal college, the Roman Pontiff. Now let us consider this problem from another angle.

The Council admitted degrees of communion with the one Church of Christ, which "subsists in" (*subsistit in*) or "stands in" the Catholic Church.[11] Sacred Scripture, the teachings of the Church Fathers and apologists, the ancient creeds, the sacraments and liturgical worship, the veneration of the saints and martyrs, the three-tiered Order and the Petrine ministry — all of these elements in the life of the ancient "undivided" Church are still to be found in the Catholic Church. The more of these elements a Christian denomination possesses, the more closely joined it is to the Catholic

---

[11] LG 8; UR 4. This formulation was purposely left vague, so as to accord better with the Catholic Church's recognition of ecclesial or Church elements in other Christian denominations. See James T. O'Connor, "The Church of Christ and the Catholic Church," in *Faith and the Sources of Faith: Proceedings of the Sixth Convention of the Fellowship of Catholic Scholars*, ed. Paul L. Williams (Scranton, Pa.: Northeast Books, 1985): 41-57.

Church. By virtue of this "ecclesiology of elements," each denomination is treated individually. Accordingly, the Orthodox and Old
Catholic Churches are in communion with the Catholic Church
to a much higher degree than the Protestant and other non-Catholic ecclesial communities and sects.[12]

The Council also acknowledged that, while the Catholic
Church possesses the fullness of truth and the means of salvation,
still "many elements of sanctification and of truth are found outside its visible confines."[13] All of these elements, "which come from
Christ and lead back to Him, belong by right to the one Church
of Christ"[14] and "bear within themselves a tendency towards unity,
having their fullness in that unity."[15] The nearly-full Catholicity (the
phrase is of course awkward) of the Eastern Churches separated

---

[12] It is fascinating and very encouraging to see how, in so many respects, Catholic and
Orthodox Christians share a common ecclesiology. One Orthodox bishop explains the
"moderate" position of his Church concerning the status of non-Orthodox: "There is
only one Church, but there are many different ways of being related to this one
Church, and many different ways of being separated from it. Some non-Orthodox are
very close indeed to Orthodoxy, others less so; some are friendly to the Orthodox
Church, others indifferent or hostile. By God's grace the Orthodox Church possesses
the fullness of truth (so its members are bound to believe), but there are other Christian
communions which possess to a greater or lesser degree a genuine measure of
Orthodoxy. All these facts must be taken into account: one cannot simply say that all
non-Orthodox are outside the Church, and leave it at that; one cannot treat other
Christians as if they stood on the same level as unbelievers." — Ware, *The Orthodox
Church*, 316.
  Of course, there are rigorists in the Orthodox Church who maintain that anyone
who is not Orthodox is wholly outside the Church; yet even the stricter group would
add that divine grace is active among non-Orthodox. The Catholic correlative of this
rigorist view was espoused by Jesuit Father Leonard Feeney; but Feeney would not
admit the possibility of salvation for non-Catholics. The "Letter of the Holy Office to
the Archbishop of Boston," dated Aug. 8, 1949, censured Feeney's position (DS 3866-
73). Recalcitrant, Feeney was excommunicated on Feb. 4, 1953, but was reconciled to
the Church shortly before his death in 1978. The correct understanding of the infallible
doctrine "*Extra Ecclesiam nulla salus*" ("No salvation outside the Church") is explained
in CCC 846-48. For a thorough study of the history of Christian thought about this
doctrine, see Francis A. Sullivan, S.J., *Salvation Outside the Church? Tracing the History
of the Catholic Response* (New York: Paulist Press, 1992).

[13] LG 8; cf. UR 3.

[14] UR 3.

[15] UUS 14.

from Rome allows an acknowledgment of the apostolic succession in them, although (from the Roman perspective) they lack the *full reality* of succession for lack of the Petrine ministry.

The ecclesiology of Vatican II offers a more generous appraisal of the communities stemming from the Protestant Reformation as well. For the dialectic of *"all or nothing"* the Council has substituted the dialectic of *"all or less."* Separated as they are from Catholic unity, many Protestant communities retain and profess a considerable part of the real Catholic faith. Despite the defects inherent in them, most notably the absence of the Eucharistic sacrifice, Catholic truths live on in them, albeit in shrivelled form and without "some contrasting and complementary element."[16]

The Holy Spirit uses the ecclesial or Catholic elements in the Protestant communities to sanctify their members.[17] Were it not for these ecclesial communities, millions would not hear of the Lord Jesus. The faith which is taught, and often the structure of these communities, is Christian as far as it goes. For reasons that are evident from the theology of Baptism, this sacrament is validly administered in Protestant communities. Consequently, where two baptized Protestants contract the bond of matrimony, the sacrament of Marriage is validly received. On the Eucharist, the Council teaches that these communities, because they lack the sacrament of Order, "have not preserved the proper reality of the Eucharistic

---

[16] Von Balthasar, *In the Fullness of Faith*, 127. Cecily Hastings would seem to be thinking along these lines when she writes in her untitled essay (in *Born Catholics*, 161-84, at 171):

> There is not a "Protestant" value within the Christian whole — divine transcendence, human helplessness, spiritual freedom, universal priesthood, or anything else — which does not turn out, in the end, to be at its strongest, wildest and richest within the ponderous machinery of the Roman Church. Not, of course, that they can be found to be so in all or in most day-to-day, would-be expositions of the Church's mind. But when, at last, one manages to get at something centrally and authentically in the full stream of her Tradition, that is what one discovers it to be.

[17] LG 15; UR 3.

mystery in its fullness."[18] What *have* they preserved then? This is a question for theologians, and leads us to the heart of the problem of the apostolic succession.

If these communities possess, to varying degrees, elements of the Eucharistic mystery, then presumably they possess a form of ministry. Bishop Kasper touches upon this when he speaks of the *vestigia* or "traces" of the Catholic Church existing in Protestant communities:

> In the same way that we find *vestigia ecclesiæ* beyond the visible limits of the Church, we also find *vestigia successionis et ministerii* beyond succession in its visible and verifiable form. With reference to the Churches of the Reform, Vatican II merely talks about a *defectus* with regard to the full form of ministry, a lack, but not a complete absence. Thus a certain degree of recognition has been conceded.[19]

The International Theological Commission (ITC) offered the same appraisal in 1973:

> [Protestant] ministers have edified and nourished their communities. By Baptism, by the study and the preaching of the word, by their prayer together and celebration of the Last Supper, and by their zeal they have guided men toward faith in the Lord and thus helped them to find the way of salvation. There are thus in such communities elements that certainly belong to the apostolicity of the unique Church of Christ.[20]

Note the acknowledgement of "a certain degree" (or vestiges) of ministry and succession in the Churches of the Reformation. What

---

[18] UR 22.

[19] Walter Kasper, Lecture, *Apostolic Succession in Episcopacy in an Ecumenical Context*, (Baltimore: St. Mary's Seminary & University, 1992), 12.

[20] "Catholic Teaching on Apostolic Succession" (1973), chap. in ITC, 93-104, quote at 104.

should be questioned and investigated more closely is: what does "a certain degree" mean?

Hardly a Catholic theologian would go so far as to say that this recognition pertains to the sacrament of Order itself (as distinct from its grace); that is, a recognition of the *res-et-signum*, the sign and hence rite, and the effect of the rite, which is the legitimate incorporation into the ecclesiastical hierarchy. Rather, it would seem that recognition pertains somehow to the grace of the sacrament (the *res sacramenti*), which is a deepening of baptismal grace in view of the specific mission of the apostolic ministry.[21] Because these denominations possess Church-traces or *vestigia* — or better yet, because the one Church of Christ is present and operative in these communities in a real albeit imperfect way — Kasper and other theologians deduce that these communities possess something which is essentially (but deficiently) ministry.[22]

Additionally, one Catholic theologian has questioned whether the quality of Protestant preaching — often considered to be better than Catholic preaching — points in favor of an authentic ministry in these communities, a ministry received without the apostolic succession but nonetheless an authentic charism of the Spirit.[23]

---

[21] Cf. Karl Rahner, ed., *Encyclopedia of Theology*, s.v. "Orders and ordination" by Piet Franzen; also Vorgrimler, 54 and 92-93.

[22] One of the earliest works to consider how schismatic Churches could be appreciated ecclesiologically is Yves Congar, *Chrétiens désunis* (Paris, 1937); English trans.: *Divided Christendom* (London, 1939). Stimulated by Congar's efforts in this area are J. Gribomont, "Du sacrement de l'Église et de ses réalisations imparfaits," *Irénikon* 22 (1949): 345-67, and C. Dumont, "Unité de l'Église et unité chrétienne," in *Les Voies de l'unité chrétienne. Doctrine et spiritualité* (Paris, 1954), 123-28. As they see it, elements or parts of the one Church are not integral parts like the districts of a town, but rather the essential whole expressing itself partially, and thus deficiently, in its powers and activities. Thus one cannot have one part without having, in some manner and to some degree, all the rest. Also Sullivan, *The Church We Believe In*, 53-55.

[23] See the doctoral thesis of Avery Dulles, "Protestant Churches and the Prophetic Office" (Diss., Woodstock College Press, 1961); also M. Villain and J. de Baciocchi, *La vocation de l'Église* (Paris, 1954), 222.

Although the Protestant minister lacks the powers of Order and jurisdiction that come with sacramental ordination,

> he is nevertheless given a *function* of preaching and he receives a gift of grace in order to lead his flock to the truth. It is not as if God wanted dissidence, but, given this dissidence, God does not abandon His People.[24]

This line of reasoning upholds the absolute sovereignty of God, whose Spirit cannot be restricted in His operation by the Church, but blows where and when He wills. Yet if we are not careful, we can make a fatal dissociation of Christ's Spirit and the Church, which is at once human and divine (even in her visibility). We must avoid an ecclesiological Nestorianism, distinguishing too emphatically between the human and divine aspects of the Church (such that her visibility is identified exclusively with her human nature).[25] Better to say that, because the Church is the Body of the Incarnate Lord which exists in time and space, the Spirit's intervention is inseparable from historical succession in office. Incarnational and pneumatic ecclesiology demand that time and space, history and Tradition, be taken seriously. Thus whatever may be said of the *res sacramenti* outside the unity of the Catholic Church (a question that deserves further theological investigation), still more is required.

---

[24] Maurice Villain, S.M., "Can There Be Apostolic Succession outside the Chain of Imposition of Hands?" *Concilium* 34 (1968): 99.

[25] Pope Pius XII's Encyclical *Mystici Corporis Christi* (June 29, 1943) dealt with this error. Cf. Henri de Lubac, "The Two Aspects of the One Church," chap. in *Splendor of the Church*, trans. Michael Mason (New York: Sheed & Ward, 1956; reprint, San Francisco: Ignatius Press, 1986), 85-125 (French: *Meditation sur L'Église* [Paris: Editions Montaigne, 1953]).

*6.3. "High" ecclesiology's problem of "apocryphal" succession*

In the nineteenth century, certain sections of Protestantism began to rediscover a sacramental outlook or *sensus*. Consequently, some denominations sought to recover the apostolic succession. Commenting on this "high-church" movement in some sectors of Protestantism, Cardinal Ratzinger writes:

> There was the longing for a link with the origins of Chris-
> tianity; a feeling of dissatisfaction with communities that
> cannot, as such, be traced back to these origins; and a need
> to demonstrate, in a visible way, their membership in the
> Church of all ages. These sentiments are, in themselves,
> perfectly legitimate and helped to break down many barri-
> ers even while being, at the same time, responsible for the
> fact that those who held ministries in these Churches man-
> aged somehow to arrange an imposition of hands by bish-
> ops who could demonstrate a connection with the imposi-
> tion of hands in the Catholic Church and were thus able to
> claim a formal legitimacy of apostolic succession. As a re-
> sult, there are, today, a number of persons holding such
> ministries whose succession is, if I may so phrase it, apoc-
> ryphal.[26]

We find "apocryphal" succession also in certain Western Churches with no historical connection to the Protestant Reformation. These Churches are determined to maintain the apostolic succession.[27]

---

[26] PCT, 245-46.

[27] To name some: the Old Catholic Church, various "national Catholic" Churches (e.g., the Polish National Catholic Church), and "traditionalist" or "integralist Catholic" groups (e.g., the Society of St. Pius X). There is even a self-designated Western Orthodox Church, which, while not recognized by the Eastern Patriarchates, nonetheless claims Apostolic Succession because its bishops trace their lineage to the Roman Catholic, Old Catholic, or Orthodox Churches. "Suffice it to say," explains Bishop C. David Luther in a promotional booklet, "that we are to the Orthodox Churches what the Eastern Rite Uniate Churches are to the Roman Catholic Church. We are an Apostolic Church. In other words, we have direct lines of episcopal

They often give the impression that what matters for them is ordination by a validly consecrated bishop, regardless of the bishop's faith and ecclesial status. The imposition of hands, in such cases, is removed from its proper ecclesial context and, as such, is grossly misunderstood. The "independent" or vagrant bishop, often without presbyters or flock of his own, is living testimony to a decadent ecclesiology. The apostolic succession is not an end in itself, but is at the service of succession in the deposit of faith. As Cardinal Ratzinger goes on:

> Wherever such "high-church" ordinations are conferred or received thus "apocryphally," the fundamental nature of the imposition of hands has been totally misunderstood. Regardless of the positive reasons that occasion it, it expresses, in such cases, either a liturgical romanticism or a canonical tutiorism. These Churches want a formally assured legitimacy and tend toward an archaizing liturgical model (often, too, toward an equally archaizing dogmatic model), but they accomplish all this without venturing to revise the ecclesial context in anything but rite. Where this occurs, however, the sacrament is, in fact, restricted to a liturgical-juridical formalism. The more genuine rite and the more genuine genealogy appear as automatic guarantors of sacramentality and apostolicity. The inevitable result is that this formalism is regarded with irony by the other side and is countered by the genuineness of the word independent of the rite.[28]

The gift of the Holy Spirit cannot be extricated from the Church which is His temple. The sacraments do not exist in isolation as private possessions, but as means of grace and salvation for the entire people of God.

---

successions leading all the way back to the apostles. And we can prove it." — *You Can Be a Priest* (Altoona, Pa.: Servants of the Good Shepherd, 1984), 9.

[28] PCT, 246

In truth, the imposition of hands with the accompanying prayer for the Holy Spirit is not a rite that can be separated from the Church or by which one can bypass the rest of the Church and dig one's own private channel to the apostles. It is, rather, an expression of the continuity of the Church, which, in the communion of the bishops, is the *locus* of Tradition, of the Gospel of Jesus Christ. Catholic theology places great emphasis on the unbroken identity of the Tradition of the apostles, which is firmly held in the unity of the concrete Church and is expressed in the ecclesial gesture of the imposition of hands. There is, in other words, no separation of the material from the formal aspect (succession in respect to the word, succession in respect to the imposition of hands); rather, its inner unity is a sign of the unity of the Church herself: the imposition of hands takes place in and lives from the Church. It is nothing without the Church — an imposition of hands that is not an entering into the existential and traditional context of the Church is not an ecclesial imposition of hands. The sacrament is the sacrament of the Church, not a private way to the beginnings of Christianity.[29]

The sacrament of Order — indeed, *every* sacrament — has its proper context only within that universal sacrament of salvation which is the Catholic Church.[30] On this point, the sacrament of Matrimony serves as an instructive analogy in at least three respects.

First, Christian marriage is a communion in life and love between husband and wife, modeled on Christ's love for His Bride the Church and instituted for the mutual support of spouses on their pilgrimage to eternal life with God. Likewise, the "pilgrim Church

---

[29] *Ibid.* For similar assessments, cf. J.M.R. Tillard, O.P., "Recognition of ministries: What is the real problem?" *One in Christ* 21 (1985): 31-39, and Villain, 87-104, esp. 94 ff.

[30] LG 48; CCC 774-76, 780; Council of Florence, *Decretum pro Iacobitis*: "For the unity of the body of the Church is of such value that the Church's sacraments are profitable to salvation only to those remaining within her" (DS 1351).

on earth"[31] is the mystery of the personal communion of each believer with the Holy Trinity and with fellow sharers in the same faith, the same sacraments and the same ecclesiastical government.[32] Secondly, the marital act both signifies and effects — like a sacrament — spousal communion. Similarly, the sacrament of Order ought to signify and effect (in addition to configuration to Christ the Priest) ecclesial communion: *symbolize*, in that the Church is never more fully united and more perfectly realized[33] than when she solemnly gathers around the one altar of the Lord (cf. 1 Cor 10:17); *effect*, in that it was principally for the perpetuation of the Eucharistic sacrifice, the true source of unity, that Christ instituted the priesthood of the bishop and his presbyters — "Do this in remembrance of Me" (Lk 22:19; cf. 1 Cor 11:25). And thirdly, just as the marital act is ordered to the procreation of new life, so ordination begets new ecclesial life (represented especially in the person of the bishop[34]) to perpetuate Christ among us.

The bishop or priest who was ordained under schism, through "apocryphal" succession, is like the child conceived outside the marital act, whether from adultery, or from fornication, or from artificial insemination: he is the product of an act removed from its proper context. Just as a child ought to be conceived from the two-in-one-flesh communion of loving spouses, so a particular Church ought to be created or perpetuated from the visible communion among the sole episcopate of the universal Church.

---

[31] Roman Missal, Eucharistic Prayer III.

[32] CCC 815, citing LG 14 and UR 2. Also UUS 9.

[33] St. Augustine, *Contra Faustum* 12.20: The Eucharist is the Sacrament "through which in the present age the Church is made" (PL 42, 265), and his *Sermo* 57.7: "For the virtue which is there understood is unity, that, built into His Body, made members of Him, we may be what we receive" (PL 38, 389); cf. St. Leo the Great, *Sermo* 63.7: "Our sharing in the Body and Blood of Christ leads to no other end than that of transforming us into that which we receive" (PL 54, 357). Cf. also LG 7; CCC 1325 and 1396.

[34] St. Cyprian, *Epist.* 66.8: "The bishop is in the Church and the Church in the bishop."

The problem with "apocryphal" ministry is that it treats succession as a self-contained principle, dissociated from ecclesial communion and Tradition. Because schism does not *of itself* incur the loss of the apostolic succession, the proper ecclesial context of Order is often disregarded. Carried to its logical extreme, what matters above all else is the "valid" reception of the sacrament of Order, even if this necessitates ordination by bishops who are outside one's own faith communion. The challenge for the Catholic Church, as Bishop Kasper sees it, is to promote an understanding of the extent to which the true nature of episcopal ministry is embedded in the context of succession-tradition-communion.[35] The apostolic succession is inseparable from the whole ecclesiality which it manifests and protects, and so ought sacramentally to express ecclesial communion in the great Tradition.

### 6.4. "Low" ecclesiology's own difficulties

"High" ecclesiology prizes the apostolic succession of bishops as a visible sign of continuity with the early Church. By contrast, the "low" ecclesiology typical of Protestantism does not consider the hierarchical descent to be an essential component of the Church's apostolicity. (This shall be made evident from the ecumenical dialogues covered in the following chapter.) If the "high" understanding of apostolicity is susceptible to abuse, nothing is to be gained by shielding the "low" view from critical analysis.

The divergent perspectives between the Catholic and Reformed Churches on the nature of ministry and the apostolic succession can be traced to the "formal principle" of the Reformation: the rejection of Tradition in favor of Scripture alone as the basis of

---

[35] Kasper, 15-16 and *passim.*

the Church's faith and life. Because the New Testament itself presents no single Church constitution as universally obligatory, "low-church" Protestantism feels free to dismiss the traditional episcopate in favor of congregationalism or presbyterianism. The Churches espousing a "high" ecclesiology, on the other hand, regard the teaching and practice of the early patristic Church as the normative interpretation of the New Testament. Consequently, they insist on the hierarchical structure of the Church, on the necessity of the apostolic succession of bishops.

Our primary interest here is the repercussions *sola Scriptura* had on ministry and Order in the Reformation Churches. The ITC wrote:

> It was a feature of the Reformation to deny the link between Scripture and Tradition and to advocate the view that Scripture alone was normative. Even if later on some sort of place for Tradition is recognized, it is never given the same position and dignity as in the ancient Church. But since the Sacrament of Orders is the indispensable sacramental expression of communion in the Tradition, the proclamation of *sola Scriptura* led inevitably to an obscuring of the older idea of the Church and its priesthood.
>
> Thus through the centuries, the imposition of hands either by men already ordained or by others was often in practice abandoned. Where it did take place, it did not have the same meaning as in the Church of Tradition. This divergence in the mode of entry into the ministry and its interpretation is only the most noteworthy symptom of the different understandings of Church and Tradition. There have already been a number of promising contacts that have sought to reestablish links with the Tradition, although the break has so far not been successfully overcome.[36]

---

[36] ITC, 103-04.

The Protestant principle of the sovereign authority of Scripture can be understood in an orthodox fashion.[37] Certainly, Church life should never contradict the biblical word of God. But the Bible cannot define everything that happens in the Church, because the Bible was written precisely out of the Church's life and is continually vivified by the Church's Tradition of preaching, worship and theology. It is from the Church that Scripture ultimately derives its authority: the Church which originally decided the canon of Scripture is the same Church which alone can interpret Scripture authoritatively. The Bible must not be regarded as something set up *over* the Church, but as something that lives and is understood *within* the Church. As the ITC writes:

> Any interpretation of Scripture that regards it as inspired and therefore normative for all ages is necessarily an interpretation that takes place within the Church's Tradition, which recognizes Scripture as inspired and normative. The recognition of the normative character of Scripture fundamentally implies a recognition of Tradition within which Scripture itself was formed and came to be considered and accepted as inspired. The normative status of Scripture and its relationship to Tradition go hand in hand. The result is that any theological considerations about Scripture are at the same time ecclesial considerations.[38]

If "high" ecclesiology's fatal attraction is to wrench tangible succession loose from communion in Church Tradition, "low" ecclesiology's proclivity is to do the same with Scripture. Père Louis

---

[37] See, for instance, the explanation given in Karl Rahner, *Foundations of Christian Faith: An Introduction to the Idea of Christianity*, trans. William V. Dych (New York: Crossroad, 1992), 361 ff. (German: *Grundkurs des Glaubens: Einführung in den Begriff des Christentums* [Freiburg im Breisgau: Verlag Herder, 1976]).

[38] ITC, 94. Along these lines is the following critique of the 1994 document *Evangelicals and Catholics Together: The Christian Mission in the Third Millennium*: "ECT 'confidently acknowledge[s] the guidance of the Holy Spirit in instances such as the

Bouyer keenly observes that the more or less absolute contradistinction in Protestantism between Scripture and Tradition has resulted in

> the more and more evident tension in Protestantism between a literalistic fundamentalism, clinging desperately, and most often vainly, to conservative formulas that serve as a support for a sincere but narrow piety, and a rationalism or liberalism that is incapable of retaining anything of the faith of the gospels, beginning with the principles that cause it to justify the rejection of Catholic Tradition.[39]

At least one Lutheran pastor concurs with Bouyer's analysis when he writes:

> The Protestant communions increasingly act like new Churches, uprooted from the Catholic Tradition and the biblical narrative. More and more, Protestantism seems unable to say why it claims what it claims or to cite compelling grounds for the position it takes. Forgetful of its Catholic roots and ambivalent about the authority of Scripture, Reformation Christianity has begun to look more and more like an empty Protestant principle, a mere negation of hierarchy and Tradition with no positive content of its own.[40]

---

formation of the canon of Scripture, the hammering out of Christological and Trinitarian doctrine in early centuries, the formulation of the Apostles' Creed as an accurate statement of scriptural truth....' For Catholic signatories these are affirmations about a specific institution (the Catholic Church) which was led by the Holy Spirit to do these very things. At the same time, Evangelical signatories credit to 'the Church' they have in mind these same accomplishments. Yet in the sense of a visible institution, the 'Church' to which the Evangelicals belong did not exist when these momentous events occurred." — Ray Ryland, "'Evangelicals and Catholics Together': A year later," *This Rock* 6 (Feb. 1995): 17. (The full text of *Evangelicals and Catholics Together* appears in *First Things* [May 1994]: 15-22.)

[39] Louis Bouyer, *Dictionary of Theology*, trans Rev. Charles Underhill Quinn (Tournai: Desclee, 1965), s.v. "Protestants."

[40] Leonard Klein, "Lutherans in Sexual Commotion," *First Things* 43 (May 1994): 35.

Liberal Protestantism needs to rediscover Scripture as the *norma normans*, the "norm that norms" Church Tradition, while Evangelical Protestantism must rediscover Scripture as the *norma normata*, the "norm that has been normed by" Tradition. Post-biblical Tradition is Scripture's proper "hermeneutical place."

*Some concluding thoughts*

The question of the apostolic succession is basically an ecclesiological question, as will be made quite evident in the following chapters. "The ecumenical problem of succession in ministry," explains Bishop Kasper, "brings us back to the central point which constitutes the unresolved fundamental problem for ecumenism to date: our understanding of the nature of the Church, of the sacramental nature of its basic structure and of its relevance for salvation."[41]

The Church is fundamentally a divine-human mystery, a Spirit-inspired sacrament. As such, she will always transcend her visible manifestations. Nonetheless, the mystery of the Church is fully realized in the communion of the Catholic Church. The visibility of this communion enables us to locate it, as well as its sacramental dimension. But one can never be certain where the Church is *not*. As St. Augustine explained, "many who appear to be outside are within," at least by implicit desire, while "many who seem to be within are outside."[42]

---

[41] Kasper, 11.
[42] *De bapt.* 5.27.38; PL 43, 195-196.

Chapter Seven

# The Ecumenical Dialogues — So Close, and Yet How Far?

Since the Second Vatican Council, several interconfessional discussions ("dialogues") have produced statements on ministry and apostolic succession. Although considerable progress has been made, it is clear that certain questions remain unresolved and require further study. By taking seriously one another's theological emphases and concerns, the Churches and ecclesial communities have been able to advance together beyond many doctrinal disagreements of the past. In this chapter we will first survey the statements produced from some of the more significant bilateral dialogues, which Pope John Paul II considers "a sure foundation for further study."[1] Then we will lead into the discussion of reunification by way of a brief commentary on the problem underlying the as-of-yet unresolved differences, namely, the problem of Tradition. The questions being asked about Tradition — what is permanently valid and binding and what is historically conditioned, what is content and what is mere formulation, and so on — can only promote the cause of Christian unity. History justifies a certain Catholic optimism about any discussion of Tradition; for critical enquiry more

---

[1] UUS 17.

often than not has led the enquirer to the fullness of Christian faith and life embodied in Catholicism. This conviction forms the basis of the last chapter of the book, which deals with the restoration of Catholic unity among all Christians.

## 7.1. Key dialogues

Following are significant bilateral statements regarding ministry and apostolic succession, presented in chronological order. Because the Catholic and Orthodox Churches have always maintained the necessity of a sacramental ministry rooted in the apostolic succession,[2] only those international dialogues between the Catholic and mainline Protestant Churches are presented here. Evidently, there has been no statement issued since the mid-1980's which said anything new about the apostolic succession specifically. Presumably, theologians have studied the apostolic succession deeply and have made it known in all its aspects: because there is really nothing new to be said about it, attention has been turned to the more fundamental problem of Tradition.

### a. Catholic/World Council of Churches Joint Theological Commission on "Catholicity and Apostolicity," "Study Document" (1970)

In the life of the Church, the apostolic preaching transmitted by Scripture and Tradition, the apostolic ministry, and life in accordance with the Gospel are inseparable. All three are essential to its apostolicity.[3]

---

[2] UUS 59, citing the Joint International Commission for Theological Dialogue between the Catholic Church and the Orthodox Church, "The Sacrament of Order in the Sacramental Structure of the Church, with Particular Reference to the Importance of Apostolic Succession for the Sanctification and Unity of the People of God" (June 26, 1988), no. 1.

[3] *One in Christ* 6 (1970): 452-83, and here at 460.

The Joint Theological Commission on "Catholicity and Apostolicity" was formed in 1967 at the request of the Joint Working Group between the Catholic Church and the World Council of Churches (WCC). In 1970, the Commission published this Study Document, which was not intended as a doctrinal consensus, "but essentially a tool in the service of joint research."[4] This passage quoted above indicates that a more comprehensive notion of apostolicity has emerged from ecumenical dialogues. Genuine apostolic succession is not defined one-sidedly as the succession of ordinations traceable to the apostles (though it certainly *does* include this), but depends also on the conformity of word and life to apostolic teaching, that is, to the Gospel.

### b. Anglican/Roman Catholic International Commission I, "Ministry and Ordination" (1973)

In the ordination of a new bishop, other bishops lay hands on him, as they request the gift of the Spirit for his ministry and receive him into their ministerial fellowship. Because they are entrusted with the oversight of other Churches, this participation in his ordination signifies that this new bishop and his Church are within the communion of Churches. Moreover, because they are representative of their Churches in fidelity to the teaching and mission of the apostles and are members of the episcopal college, their participation also ensures the historical continuity of this Church with the apostolic Church and of its bishop with the original apostolic ministry. The communion of the Churches in mission, faith, and holiness, through time and space, is thus symbolized and maintained in the bishop. Here are comprised the essential features of what is meant in our two traditions by ordination in the apostolic succession.[5]

---

[4] *Ibid.*, 453.
[5] No. 16, in Anglican/Roman Catholic International Commission, *The Final Report* (Cincinnati: Forward Movement Publications; Washington: U.S. Catholic Conference, 1982), 37-38.

Anglicans and Catholics have been meeting in official consultations at the international level since 1970. The first ongoing forum for international dialogue, called the Anglican/Roman Catholic International Commission (ARCIC), held thirteen plenary sessions from 1970 to 1981, producing four *Statements* and three sets of *Elucidations*. All agreed Statements and Elucidations were compiled and published in 1981 under the title, *The Final Report*. A second forum, ARCIC-II, started in 1983.

Vatican II referred to the Anglican Communion as occupying a "special place" among the denominations issuing from the Reformation.[6] Unlike the other Reformation bodies, the Anglican Communion has always maintained the necessity of preserving continuity with the apostolic Church through the succession of episcopal ordinations. Anglicanism also parts company with the rest of Protestantism in recognizing the true sacramentality of ordination.[7] Difficulties arise, however, as to the validity of Anglican Orders — a matter so complex that it cannot here be pursued at length.[8] The ordination of women in several Anglican Churches has added a new level of complexity, practically halting reunion negotiations with the Catholic and Orthodox Churches alike.[9]

---

[6] UR 13.

[7] *Ministry and Ordination; Elucidation* (1979), no. 3, in *The Final Report*, 42.

[8] See Chapter 8.1.B, fn. 19.

[9] The ordination of women poses a serious ecumenical problem, especially in view of Pope John Paul II's reaffirmation of the Catholic Church's position. In his Apostolic Letter *Ordinatio Sacerdotalis* (May 30, 1994), the Pontiff pronounced that "the Church has no authority whatsoever to confer priestly ordination on women, and that this judgment is to be definitively held by all the Church's faithful" (no. 4). The ordination of women in the Anglican Church and in other ecclesial communities would now seem to pose an insurmountable obstacle to full unity, since it is unlikely that many women ministers would be willing to enter the Catholic Church as laywomen, without possibility of priestly ordination.

An interesting treatise on the place of women in the Church is Louis Bouyer, "A Female Priesthood?" chap. in *Woman in the Church*, trans. Marilyn Teichert (San Francisco: Ignatius Press, 1979) (French: *Mystère et ministère de la femme dans l'église* [Paris: Aubier, 1976]). An exhaustive study of the question from the perspectives of

The apostolic succession is not dealt with directly in the *Final Report* of ARCIC-I, but it is referred to in *Ministry and Ordination*, no. 16 (quoted above), and in its *Elucidation*, no. 4. The essential features of "what is meant in our two traditions by ordination in the apostolic succession" are set down in MO 16. The official Catholic Response to the *Final Report*, while generally favorable, states that "further clarification" is needed from the Catholic perspective before the Report can be considered as corresponding fully to Catholic doctrine on ordained ministry. With regard to the Statement and Elucidation on *Ministry and Ordination*, the Response notes that

> the Catholic Church recognizes in the apostolic succession both an unbroken line of episcopal ordination from Christ through the apostles down through the centuries to the bishops of today, and an uninterrupted continuity in Christian doctrine from Christ to those today who teach in union with the College of Bishops and its head, the Successor of Peter.[10]

---

anthropology, biology, psychology, philosophy and theology is Manfred Hauke, *Women in the Priesthood? A Systematic Analysis in Light of the Order of Creation and Redemption*, trans. David Kipp (San Francisco: Ignatius Press, 1988).

Some contend that the priestly ordination of women remains open to discussion, and will remain open until it is definitively settled by the exercise of papal infallibility. It can be soundly argued that this teaching is already infallible, according to the four criteria of infallibility specified in Vatican I's Dogmatic Constitution *Pastor Æternus* (DS 3074) and reiterated in LG 25. The Pope states that he is speaking in view of his Petrine ministry to confirm the brethren (Lk 22:32), thus fulfilling the condition (1) that the Pope speak "by virtue of his supreme apostolic authority," in his capacity "as pastor and teacher of all Christians. . ." Furthermore, the subject concerns the "matter" of a sacrament and thus meets the condition (2) that the issue relate to faith or morals. Finally, the Pope states "that this judgment is to be held by all the Church's faithful," thus satisfying the criteria (3) that the doctrine put forth be "required to be held by the whole Church," and (4) that the Pope "define" the doctrine in question, pronouncing directly and conclusively. On Nov. 18, 1995, the Vatican Congregation for the Doctrine of the Faith released a *Responsum* (dated Oct. 28, 1995) affirming that the Church's teaching against ordaining women to the priesthood must be understood as part of the deposit of faith, and therefore as infallible.

[10] Pontifical Council for Promoting Christian Unity, *Information Service*, no. 82 (1993): 47-51.

Thereafter the Response cites article 20 of *Lumen Gentium* at length,[11] in order to affirm the causal relationship between the unbroken lines of episcopal succession and apostolic doctrine.

### c. Methodist/Catholic Conversations, "Dublin Report" (1976)

For Roman Catholics the graded threefold ministry is derived from the teaching of the New Testament through the living Tradition of the Church. True succession in ministry is guaranteed only by episcopal laying-on of hands in historical succession and authentic transmission of the Faith within the apostolic college.

Methodists hold that the New Testament does not lay down any one form of ministry as binding for all times and places, and therefore the single form of ministry which British Methodists and other non-episcopal Churches have is at least as consonant with the presbyter-bishops of the New Testament as the threefold ministry is. Methodists have no difficulty in accepting as true ministries those which emerged at the Reformation and in the eighteenth century, so long as they are faithful to New Testament ministry. They accept, however, the appropriateness of the threefold ministry of other Churches for a united Church....

Moreover Methodists, both British and American, preserve a form of ministerial succession in practice and can regard a succession of ordination from the earliest times as a valuable *symbol* of the Church's continuity with the Church of the New Testament, though they would not use it as a *criterion*.[12]

Since its beginning in 1967 under the auspices of the World Methodist Council, this dialogue has produced general surveys dealing with a variety of topics every five years. The second plenary meeting of the WMC was held in Dublin in 1976. The Dublin

---

[11] See Chapter 5.3 for the relevant text of LG 20.
[12] Nn. 85-87, in GiA, 358.

Report indicates that, while Methodists do not reject the three-ordered ministry as unscriptural, neither do they regard it essential to the Church's constitution. Moreover, the position that material succession from the ancient Church is a *symbol*, though not a *criterion*, of apostolicity, is one that is shared with other Protestant denominations.

### d. Roman Catholic/Presbyterian-Reformed Consultation, "The Unity We Seek" (1977)

The Church is apostolic in that it lives the faith of the apostles and continues the mission which Christ gave to the apostles. The canonical Scriptures are the normative expression of this apostolicity. Within the general ministry of the whole Church the setting apart of some to the administration of the Word and sacrament includes the invocation of the Holy Spirit and the laying-on of hands by other ordained ministers. The continuity of this special ministry of Word and sacrament arises in Christ's original commission to the apostles but depends also on His continual call and action. The invocation of the Holy Spirit reminds us that Jesus Christ is present and at work through the continual operation of His Holy Spirit. The laying-on of hands is an effective sign that initiates and confirms the believer in the ministry which is conferred.

We believe in apostolic succession within the Church, though from our different standpoints we locate that succession in different ways. Apostolic succession consists at least in the continuity of the apostles' teaching, and this understanding is not in opposition to the idea of succession through continuity of ordained ministry. The two elements already described both inhere in apostolic succession: historical continuity with the apostles and the contemporary action of Christ through the Holy Spirit.[13]

---

[13] Bishop Ernest L. Unterkoefler and Dr. Andrew Harsanyi, eds., *The Unity We Seek. A Statement by the Roman Catholic/Presbyterian-Reformed Consultation* (New York: Paulist Press, 1977), 31-32.

This statement synthesizes the agreements reached between Catholics and Presbyterians in several bilateral consultations held between 1965 and 1975. The orthodox Catholic can scarcely take issue with this declaration, because the "high-church" stress on juridico-sacramental succession and the "low-church" stress on doctrinal succession are both upheld as important to apostolicity. Moreover, the apostolic succession is entered through the imposition of hands by one already ordained. The ordained are called by Christ and empowered for the ministry by the Holy Spirit at work in and through the Church.

*e. World Alliance of Reformed Churches/Vatican Secretariat for Promoting Christian Unity, "The Presence of Christ in Church and World" (1977)*

There are several senses of "apostolic succession"; but when it is taken in its usual meaning to refer to the continuity of the special ministry, clearly it occurs within the apostolicity which belongs to the whole Church. Reformed and Roman Catholic both believe that there is an apostolic succession essential to the life of the Church, though we locate that succession differently. We agree that no one assumes a special ministry solely on personal initiative, but enters into the continuous special ministry of Word and sacrament through the calling of the community and the act of ordination by other ministers.

Apostolic succession consists at least in continuity of apostolic doctrine; but this is not in opposition to succession through continuity of ordained ministry. The continuity of right doctrine is guarded by the application of Holy Scripture and transmitted by the continuity of the teaching function of the special ministry. As with all aspects of the Church's ministry, so with the particular case of apostolic succession: it requires at once a historical continuity with the original apostles and a contemporary and graciously re-

newed action of the Holy Spirit. The Church lives by the
continuity of the free gift of the Spirit according to Christ's
promises, and this excludes a ritualistic conception of succession, the conception of mechanical continuity, a succession divorced from the historical continuity.[14]

One of the most important international bilateral dialogues has been
that between the World Alliance of Reformed Churches and the
Vatican Secretariat for Promoting Christian Unity. After five an-
nual meetings, the participants in this dialogue published their final
report in 1977, entitled *The Presence of Christ in Church and World*
(PCCW). The quotation above is taken from the last part of the
report, on the topic of ministry. Notice how strikingly similar the
language of PCCW is to that of the Roman Catholic/Presbyte-
rian-Reformed Consultation's document, *The Unity We Seek*
(above). Both statements present a balanced and comprehensive
notion of apostolicity which takes into account faithfulness in doctrine, ministry, sacrament and life. Furthermore, both this statement and *The Unity We Seek* note that the Catholic and Reformed
traditions locate apostolic succession in different ways; yet to ac-
centuate one aspect of succession is not to dismiss the others.
PCCW does, however, quite clearly reject what we have been calling "apocryphal" succession. While apostolicity does not permit
"succession divorced from the historical continuity" (an agreement
which should goad the Protestant communities to reinsert themselves into the historical episcopate), neither does it allow for a
purely "mechanical continuity" which lacks ecclesiological reference
(i.e., "apocryphal" succession).

---

[14] No. 101, in GiA, 457-58.

## f. Lutheran/Roman Catholic Joint Commission,
### "The Ministry in the Church" (1981)

The most important question regarding the theology of the episcopal office and regarding the mutual recognition of ministries is the problem of the apostolic succession. This is normally taken to mean the unbroken ministerial succession of bishops in a Church. But apostolic succession is also often understood to refer in the substantive sense to the apostolicity of the Church in faith…. In the New Testament and in the period of the early Fathers, the emphasis was placed more on the substantive understanding of the apostolic succession in faith and life. The Lutheran tradition speaks in this connection of a *successio verbi*. In present-day Catholic theology, more and more often the view is adopted that the substantive understanding of apostolicity is primary. Far-reaching agreement on this understanding of apostolic succession is therefore developing.

As regards the succession of ministers, the joint starting point for both Catholics and Lutherans is that there is an integral relation between the witness of the Gospel and witnesses to the Gospel.[15] The witness to the Gospel has been entrusted to the Church as a whole. Therefore, the whole Church as the *ecclesia apostolica* stands in the apostolic succession. Succession in the sense of the succession of ministers must be seen within the succession of the whole Church in the apostolic Faith.[16]

This international dialogue began in 1965. Its first document, *The Gospel and the Church* (1972), sometimes called "the Malta

---

[15] Cf. Lutheran/Roman Catholic Joint Commission's "Malta Report" (1972), no. 48, in GiA, 179.

[16] Nn. 59-61, in GiA, 266-67. Cf. the similar view of the Orthodox: "The relation between the bishop and his flock is a mutual one. The bishop is the divinely appointed *teacher* of the faith, but the *guardian* of the faith is not the episcopate alone, but the whole people of God, bishops, clergy, and laity together. The proclamation of the truth is not the same as the possession of the truth: all the people possess the truth, but it is the bishop's particular office to proclaim it." — Ware, *The Orthodox Church*, 255.

Report," presents an overview of traditional questions dividing the Catholic and Lutheran Churches, with an indication of the evolution of these topics since the Reformation. In 1981 the Commission published *The Ministry in the Church*. One reason for "far-reaching agreement" is that Catholics and Lutherans are taking seriously each side's legitimate concerns. Cognizant of the problem of "apocryphal" succession, Catholics are aware of the need to keep historical succession at the service of apostolic witness and fellowship. Lutherans, for their part, have come to realize that the legitimate preaching of apostolic doctrine and the administration of sacraments would have to be a function of a ministerial office deriving from Christ and the apostles. Consequently, both sides agree that there is an "integral relationship" between the legitimacy of the Gospel that is preached and the legitimacy of its preachers.

### g. WCC Faith and Order Commission, "Lima Report" (1982)

In the Creed, the Church professes itself to be apostolic. The Church lives in continuity with the apostles and their proclamation. The same Lord Who sent the apostles continues to be present in the Church. The Spirit keeps the Church in the apostolic Tradition until the fulfillment of history in the Kingdom of God. Apostolic Tradition in the Church means continuity in the permanent characteristics of the Church of the apostles: witness to the apostolic Faith, proclamation and fresh interpretation of the Gospel, celebration of Baptism and the Eucharist, the transmission of ministerial responsibilities, communion in prayer, love, joy and suffering, service to the sick and the needy, unity among the local Churches and sharing the gifts which the Lord has given to each...[17]

Among the issues that need to be worked on as Churches move towards mutual recognition of ministries, that of ap-

---

[17] No. 34, in GiA, 491.

ostolic succession is of particular importance. Churches in ecumenical conversations can recognize their respective ordained ministries if they are mutually assured of their intention to transmit the ministry of Word and sacrament in continuity with apostolic times. The act of transmission should be performed in accordance with the apostolic Tradition, which includes the invocation of the Spirit and the laying-on of hands.

In order to achieve mutual recognition, different steps are required of different Churches. For example:

a) Churches which have preserved the episcopal succession are asked to recognize both the apostolic content of the ordained ministry which exists in Churches which have not maintained such succession and also the existence in these Churches of a ministry of *episkopé* in various forms.

b) Churches without the episcopal succession, and living in faithful continuity with the apostolic Faith and mission, have a ministry of Word and sacrament, as is evident from the belief, practice and life of those Churches. These Churches are asked to realize that the continuity with the Church of the apostles finds profound expression in the successive laying-on of hands by bishops and that, though they may not lack the continuity of the apostolic Tradition, this sign will strengthen and deepen that continuity. They may need to recover the sign of the episcopal succession.[18]

In 1982, the Faith and Order Commission of the World Council of Churches published an agreement entitled, *Baptism, Eucharist, and Ministry*, often called "the Lima Report," from the Peruvian capital where it was released. The Lima Report encapsulates the furthest advance towards Catholicity heretofore made by the generality of the Protestant communities.

The official Catholic Response to the Lima Report, sent to the WCC in August 1987, was given its final form in collabora-

---

[18] Nn. 52-53, in GiA, 494-95.

tion between the Secretariat for Promoting Christian Unity and the Congregation for the Doctrine of the Faith. The Response praises the Report's appreciation of Catholic positions, the weight it gives to sacred Tradition, and the theological depth at which most questions are treated. At the same time, it indicates several areas that stand in need of further clarification. Concerning ministry and the apostolic succession, the Catholic Church is not content to leave unsettled the question whether or not ordination is a sacrament. The Response states:

> We agree that the "episcopal succession" is of the order of the sign that can signify, through the image of historical transmission, the fact that the Church is rooted in the apostolic Church around Christ and therefore shows its fundamental apostolicity. However, the meaning of "sign/expression" needs to be clear. In the previous version, *One Baptism, One Eucharist and a Mutually Recognized Ministry* (no. 34), the text spoke of an "effective sign." This indicates better the unique importance of the episcopal succession for the edification of the Church through the ages. This is immediately related to the meaning which the ministry of the bishop has in a Catholic ecclesiology: it is more than a function of oversight next to other functions and ministries. In his very personal ministry, the bishop represents the local Church entrusted to him. He is its qualified spokesperson in the communion of the Churches. At the same time, he is the first representative of Jesus Christ in the community. By this ordination to the episcopacy, he is commissioned to exercise leadership in the community, to teach with authority and to judge. All other ministries are linked to his and function in relationship to it. Thus his ministry is a sacramental sign of integration and a focus of communion. Through the episcopal succession, the bishop embodies and actualizes both catholicity in time, i.e., the continuity of the Church across the generations, as well as the communion lived in each generation. The actual community is thus

linked up through a personal sign with the apostolic origins, its teaching and way of living.[19]

Furthermore, the Response takes exception with the Lima Report's failure to illustrate adequately the interrelatedness of the apostolic succession and Tradition:

> The connection of the apostolic succession with the apostolic Tradition, understood as "the continuity in the permanent characteristics of the Church of the apostles," in their witness, proclamation, celebration, service, etc. (no. 34), is legitimate. One may even say as in no. 36: "The succession of bishops became one of the ways, together with the transmission of the Gospel and the life of the community, in which the apostolic Tradition of the Church was expressed." But is there not the tendency here to be content with a listing and a juxtaposition of items which all have to do with the apostolic Tradition without showing sufficiently how they have their own function within the totality and how they are related among themselves?[20]

From the Catholic perspective, the episcopal succession not only serves and guards the Tradition, but is also a component of Tradition. The reciprocal recognition of ministries, as called for by this document, would have to depend on the resolution of this problem. "It is not only agreement on the question of apostolic succession," say the Catholic respondents, "but also being situated within it that is necessary for recognition of ordination."

---

[19] *Origins* 17 (1987): 401, 403-16, quote at 414.

[20] *Ibid.*, 413-14. The Catholic Response appears also in *Churches Respond to "Baptism, Eucharist and Ministry" Text* I, ed. Max Thurian (Geneva: WCC [coll. Faith and Order Paper No. 144], 1988); and *Baptism, Eucharist and Ministry, 1982-1990. Report on the Processes and Responses* (Geneva: WCC [coll. Faith and Order Paper No. 149], 1992). Two years before the official Catholic response, Edward J. Kilmartin, S.J., neatly summarized the points of agreement and divergence in his own evaluation of BEM: "A Catholic Response to Lima 1982," *One in Christ* 21 (1985): 204-16.

### h. Lutheran/Roman Catholic Joint Commission, "Facing Unity" (1985)

Lutherans, like Catholics, can recognize as "the action of the Spirit"[21] the historical differentiation of the one apostolic ministry into more local ministry and more regional forms, and they can consider "the function of *episcopè...* as necessary for the Church."[22] Likewise, Lutherans feel free "to face up to the call for communion with the historic episcopal office,"[23] i.e., the historically evolved pattern of episcopal ministry in the form of the office of bishop standing in apostolic succession. Nevertheless, Lutherans and Catholics place different accents on the significance of that historic episcopal office for the Church.

The two problems are closely related: The "lack of the sacrament of Orders" that the Catholic side claims to be inherent in the ministry of the Lutheran Churches cannot, because of its very nature, be annulled solely by theological insights and agreements or by ecclesiastical or canonical declarations and decisions, as, for example, by the theological and canonical act of recognizing these ministries. What is needed, rather, is acceptance of the fellowship in ecclesial ministry, and this, ultimately, means acceptance of the fellowship in episcopal ministry which stands in apostolic succession. Lutherans are fundamentally free and open to accept such fellowship in the episcopal office. Yet within this understanding of the importance or significance of the episcopal office for the catholicity, apostolicity and unity of the Church, Lutherans are inclined to place the accent differently from Catholics.

The problems mentioned here need not block the road to fellowship in the Church ministry and therefore to a fully structured ecclesial fellowship. But it does call for renewal and deepening of the understanding of the ordained min-

---

[21] "The Ministry of the Church," no. 45, in GiA, 263.
[22] *Ibid.*, no. 43, in GiA, 263.
[23] *Ibid.*, no. 80, in GiA, 273.

istry, particularly the ministry serving the unity and governance (*episkopê*) of the Church.[24]

In 1985, the Lutheran/Roman Catholic Joint Commission wrote *Facing Unity* in an attempt to foresee and outline the possible ways in which the full reconciliation of Lutherans and Catholics can take place. As with *The Ministry in the Church* (1981), we find in *Facing Unity* that Catholics and Lutherans agree on the value of the episcopal office, yet there is disagreement about its importance for apostolicity. While "open" to hierarchical communion with the Catholic episcopate, Lutherans nonetheless maintain that their ministries are apostolic, and therefore valid, because (in their view) the historical episcopate is not essential to apostolicity. Catholics, on the other hand, insist that episcopal ordination is the indispensable form for the transmission of the apostolic succession.

Even if these differences are resolved, consensus statements cannot suffice to bring about reunion. What is needed first, *Facing Unity* insists, is "acceptance of the fellowship in ecclesial ministry." On the Catholic side, Kilmartin holds the same opinion:

> Can these Churches, which are asked to introduce the episcopacy, come to a correct experience of an episcopally constituted Church without experiencing in practice communion with episcopally constituted Churches, even before they have accepted this constitution as pertaining to more than the *bene esse* of the Church? Could the Catholic Church go along with the recommendation of episcopal constitution for Churches which lack it without supporting their experience by concrete visible expressions of communion on the way to full communion?[25]

Such a recommendation, perhaps, is best considered in the light of

---

[24] Secretariat for Promoting Christian Unity, *Information Service*, no. 59 (1985): 44-72, quote at 60.

[25] Kilmartin, 216.

what Cardinal Ratzinger said about the mutual recognition of ministries: "Unification requires of the whole faith community a thorough state of inner readiness for which neither theological nor ecclesiological authority is an adequate substitute."[26]

## 7.2. Tradition: problem or opportunity?

As noted at the beginning of this chapter, since the 1980's nothing really novel has been said in ecumenical dialogues on the apostolic succession. What seems to occupy the theologians involved in ecumenical dialogue nowadays is the problem of Tradition: where does the Christian Tradition mark the parameters of legitimate theological pluralism? which differences among the Churches are tolerable and which are intolerable? is Tradition's object-content coextensive with Scripture? how to distinguish the truth from historical developments which are closely related to the truth?

These questions are motivated by a desire to determine which of the two basic forms of Western Christianity, Roman Catholic or Reformed, better represents the great and permanently valid Tradition. Does Evangelical Christianity, as the adjective denotes, embody the apostolic Tradition more faithfully than Catholicism? Have the Reformation Churches preserved the apostolicity of the Church even in its "low" sense, that is, as apostolicity of faith? If we are to make progress along these lines, we must of course look to the faith and life of the primitive Church. Fear of history has proved a poor counsellor to ecclesiology and to theology in general. It does not seem out of place, then, to consider just a few points of doctrine which have typically divided Catholicism and Protestantism:

---

[26] PCT, 218-19.

* Did the early Church understand herself to be an *invisible fellowship*, or a *visible communion*?
* Was Baptism regarded as merely *testimony to* regeneration, or as the *sacrament of* regeneration?
* Did the early Christians celebrate the Lord's Supper simply as a *memorial meal*, or as the *sacrificial banquet* of the Lord's Body and Blood?
* Were the sacraments ("mysteries," as they are called in Byzantine Christianity) held to be *mere symbols* of grace, or were they regarded as *channels* of grace?

Of course this account of differences is far from complete; nor is the disparity between positions so sharp as to merit the "or" in the above formulations. Nevertheless, these points of doctrine need to be considered in order to assess whether the apostolic spirit and ministry is embodied more purely in Catholic or in Protestant Christianity. Karl Rahner's cornments on this matter are worth citing:

> For Evangelical Christianity to prove its own historical and theological continuity with the ancient Church, it must declare a great deal in this earlier, pre-Reformation Church to be either superfluous or even un-Christian and anti-Christian. We can say that at least with regard to the episcopal constitution of the Church, with regard to the normal and evident transmission of this episcopacy, and with regard to the Petrine office, the more self-evident, more unbroken and more directly transmitted continuity exists between the ancient Church and the Church of post-Tridentine Catholicism. Something similar can also be said for many other things, for example, with regard to law and with regard to sacramental practice.[27]

---

[27] Karl Rahner, "Christianity as Church," chap. in *Foundations of Christian Faith*, 322-401, quote at 357-58.

This was precisely the discovery made by the Venerable John
Henry Newman while he was Anglican. Anyone who studies the
patristic age cannot but conclude that the history of the development of doctrine[28] supports the continuity of what is today commonly (though not quite correctly) called the "Roman Catholic
Church"[29] with the Church of the early centuries, the Church de-

---

[28] The development of doctrine is central to the question of Tradition. Karl Adam's
succinct explanation is helpful: "Christian revelation, the mystery of the crucified God,
was and is something whole and complete, ended by the death of the last apostle, even
though the entire content of its truth may not be explicitly displayed in all its fullness,
but lies nestling like a closed bud in the Church's consciousness of her revealing power"
— "Christ and the Western Mind," in *Two Essays*, trans. Edward Bullough (London:
Sheed & Ward, 1930), 14.

  And Küng writes: "Truth must be rediscovered, reconquered anew in every age.
Truths cannot be handed on like bricks, preferably undisturbed. Truth is not like stone,
it is a thing of the spirit which is lost if it is allowed to petrify. Even dogmas and
articles of faith are not frozen or petrified formulas, set apart from the course of human
history. They too originated in specific historical situations and must constantly be
prised out of their historical setting and put in wider (but of course still finite) historical
perspective, so that we can appreciate them correctly, more fully, more truly" — *The
Church*, 290.

[29] The term "Roman Catholic" is used advisedly. (See the easily comprehensible articles
by John J. Moran, "Catholic or Roman Catholic?" *The Catholic Answer* 6 [Jan./Feb.
1993]: 46-49; and Kenneth D. Whitehead, "How Did the Catholic Church Get Her
Name?" *The Catholic Answer* 9 [May/June 1995]: 56-59.) The name is of relatively
recent origin, having been coined by proponents of "high-church" Anglicanism's
Branch Theory. According to this theory, the Catholic Church is comprised of three
co-equal branches or communions: the Roman, the Anglican and the Orthodox: the
Pope heads the Roman branch only, i.e., the See of Rome and the particular Churches
under its patriarchal jurisdiction.

  The element of truth in this beguiling theory is that the Roman Church does
recognize the Catholicity of many non-Roman Churches (see OE 2-3, on the Eastern
Catholic Churches); however, these Churches are Catholic because they have preserved
the fullness of apostolic Tradition, which includes communion with the successor of
Peter (cf. LG 22). Having become convinced that the Anglican Church was no longer
Catholic and Apostolic, but rather national and peculiar, Newman disavowed the
Branch Theory and entered the Catholic Church in 1845, at great (temporal) cost to
him.

  Because the Orthodox Church believes herself to be the true Catholic Church —
from the East's point of view, Rome gradually departed from Catholic unity —
Orthodox, too, speak of the "Roman Catholic" Church in contradistinction to the
"Orthodox Catholic" Church. Not surprisingly, Orthodox apologists reject the Branch
Theory for the same reason Catholics reject it, namely: because full Catholicity
constitutes membership in the true Church. Bishop Kallistos (Timothy) Ware, a
convert to Orthodoxy from Anglicanism, explains: "If we are going to speak in terms of

scribed by Irenaeus, Ignatius of Antioch, Clement of Rome, and Justin the Martyr. Newman wrote in 1850:

> No other form of Christianity but this present Catholic Communion, has a pretence to resemble, even in the faintest shadow, the Christianity of Antiquity, viewed as a living religion on the stage of the world.... You may take ten thousand extracts from the Fathers, and not get deeper into the state of their times than the paper you write upon; to imbibe into the Ancient Church as a fact, is either to be a Catholic or an infidel.[30]

The "low-church" idea of a spiritual apostolicity without the episcopal office is simply too formless, too unreal, for Henri de Lubac. In his reflections on the Church, published in the early 1950's, the renowned theologian (and later cardinal) wrote:

> If anyone can extract a clear-cut meaning from the term "apostolicity of the spirit" — as opposed to any idea of historic succession — he is welcome to do so. The matter has, in any case, never been viewed thus, from the very first. And it seems preferable by far to believe St. Irenaeus when he

---

'branches', then from the Orthodox point of view the only branches which the Catholic Church can have are the local Autocephalous Churches of the Orthodox communion." — *The Orthodox Church*, 251.

Orthodox would agree that the catholicity of the Church requires the recognition of the primacy of Peter's successor, but they differ with Rome on what primacy means concretely. By recovering the ecclesiology of *communio*, Vatican II corrected certain imbalances in Latin Catholic ecclesiology, thus narrowing the gap between East and West (cf. John Meyendorff, *Catholicity and the Church* [Crestwood, N.Y.: St. Vladimir's Seminary Press, 1983], 97 ff.). "Orthodox in their turn," Ware remarks (*The Orthodox Church*, 323), "need to take the idea of Primacy more seriously. Orthodox agree that the Pope is first among bishops: have they asked themselves carefully and searchingly what this really means?" Also see Miller, "The Papacy and the East," chap. in *The Shepherd and the Rock*, 115 ff.

[30] *The Works of Cardinal Newman*, vol. 5, *Certain Difficulties Felt by Anglicans in Catholic Teaching*, 2 vols., new ed. (Westminster, Md.: Christian Classics, 1969), 1:393. Newman reiterates this conviction throughout his work.

depicts the apostles as entrusting to bishops the Churches which were entrusted to themselves.[31]

Notwithstanding the abuse of "apocryphal" succession, the tangible apostolic succession should not be dismissed as mechanistic or legalistic.

A real, uninterrupted continuity in faith and Order unites the Catholic Church to the first Christian disciples, to the "root of Christian society."[32] It is in this frame of mind that we are now ready to consider some proposals for restoring full, visible communion among the disparate Churches.

---

[31] Henri de Lubac, S.J., *The Splendor of the Church*, translated by Michael Mason (New York: Sheed & Ward, 1956; reprinted San Francisco: Ignatius Press, 1986), 87-88, citing Irenaeus, *Adv. Hær.* 5.2.1: "The bishops, to whom the apostles handed over the Churches..." (PG 7, 1177a).

[32] St. Augustine, *Epist.* 232.3: "You certainly see many have gone before from the root of Christian society, which is spread throughout the world by a sure propagation through the Sees of the apostles and the successions of bishops" (PL 33, 1028); *Contra Faustum* 11.2 (PL 42, 246), 28.2 (PL 33, 486), etc. Cf. Dom T. Belpaire, O.S.B., "Autonomie et unité ecclésiologique," *Irénikon* (1949): 58.

Chapter Eight

# The Reunification of the
# Churches — Some Speculation

The one ultimate desire of ecumenism, Pope John Paul II reminds us in his Encyclical *Ut Unum Sint*, "is to reestablish full visible unity among all the baptized."[1] "Full unity will come about when all share in the fullness of the means of salvation entrusted by Christ to His Church."[2] Because that fullness is already present in the Catholic Church,[3] the final goal of ecumenism (as Catholics see it) can be nothing less than the return or reconciliation of all Christians to Catholic Christianity. The realization of this goal requires that we deal with the problem of non-Catholic ministries. If in the future a separated community were to embrace the Catholic faith, how might it be integrated into the Catholic Church?

The first section of this chapter presents some proposals for reunion, touching upon some of the difficulties involved in each proposal. These proposals concern only those ecclesial communities outside the episcopal succession, most of which come under the general heading "Protestant." In view of the attention given to orthopraxy nowadays, the second section offers a proposal for preserving the intrinsic unity of sacramental ordination and visible

---

[1] UUS 77.
[2] UUS 86.
[3] LG 8; UR 3.

communion in the Church's Tradition. This proposal springs from the conviction that the Church's practice with regard to sacramental recognition should reflect her theology of the sacrament of Order — a theology which does not dissociate the sacrament either from the one apostolic Tradition or from hierarchical communion. Doctrine and practice are inseparable.

## 8.1. Proposals for restoring full communion following doctrinal consensus

When an ordained minister of a Christian denomination outside the historical apostolic succession comes into full communion with the Catholic Church, it is the current practice of the Church to receive him or her as a layperson. Assuming their vocation is authenticated by the external call of the Church, the sacrament of Order is conferred on those men who might wish to continue their pastoral office as Catholics. From the viewpoint of the Catholic Church, this is not re-ordination (which, sacramentally speaking, is impossible), but ordination. There is the possibility of conditional ordination for some.[4] Let us consider some alternative possibilities for restoring visible communion in the event that the Catholic Church and another communion were to reach full agreement in faith.

---

[4] Such was the case with Dr. Graham Leonard, retired Anglican Bishop of London, who was received into the Catholic Church on April 6, 1994. Later that month, on April 23, Basil Cardinal Hume conditionally ordained Dr. Leonard to the priesthood. In the ordination liturgy, the cardinal used the words, *"si non es iam valide ordinatus..."* ("If you are not already validly ordained..."). This formula was possible because Dr. Leonard, who was averse to denying his former ministry, provided the Holy see with detailed documentation testifying to the matter, form and intention of the Anglican bishops in the Old Catholic lineage who took part in his priestly and episcopal ordinations. Nonetheless, "a prudent doubt" justified the conditional ordination. Father Leonard commented that not all Anglican clergy seeking communion with Rome should expect similar treatment. — Kevin Grant, "If..." *Catholic World Report*, June 1994: 16.

### a. A diversity of polities within the one Church?

Brown suggests the possibility of reunion without assimilating the non-Catholic clergy into the Catholic hierarchy through sacramental ordination. He entertains the idea of episcopal and non-episcopal Churches coexisting in the communion of the one Church:

> The likelihood that in Paul's lifetime some of his Churches that had no bishops lived in fellowship with Churches that had bishops suggests the possibility of two such Churches living in union today. The probability that not all the presbyter-bishops of the years 80-110 could trace their position back to appointment or ordination by an apostle suggests the possibility of our openness to Churches with an episcopate that (by our standards) is not in historical succession to the apostles.[5]

In other words, given the plurality of configurations in the primitive Church (the monepiscopate was not universal until the second century), the reunified Church would not commit herself to any particular constitution incumbent upon all the particular or local Churches. Congregational, presbyterian and episcopalian polities would all have a place in the Church, so long as the particular Churches agree with one another on doctrinal and moral essentials. How does this scheme stand up to Catholic ecclesiology?

Brown correctly points out that reconciliation need not necessarily involve absorption. In all reunion discussions, Catholics are guided by the principle of "full unity in legitimate diversity."[6] There

---

[5] Brown, *Priest and Bishop*, 83.

[6] UUS 57. Hence, Catholic ecumenists are swift to assure their non-Catholic colleagues that "full ecclesial communion" does not demand melding the separated Churches into a "megachurch," and point out the Eastern Churches in union with Rome. Looking to the future, then, some maintain that the restoration of the separated Western Churches and ecclesial communities to full Catholic unity should not entail their absorption into the Roman Church. (See Fr. John Hotchkin, "The Ecumenical Movement's Third Stage," *Origins* 25 [1995]: 353, 355-61.)

is no need to impose a rigid uniformity on all alike. The Catholic Church is a communion of particular Churches using a diversity of liturgical rites, theological traditions, canonical disciplines, and even (to some measure) systems of outward organization. However, when we speak of the Catholic Church as a communion of Churches, we do not mean that the Church is simply the sum of the particular Churches, or a federation of particular Churches. Ecclesial communion is not quantitative. Catholics who appreciate Vatican II's revival of the ancient *communio* ecclesiology should have no quarrel with the Orthodox theologian who remarked:

> 'One plus one is still *one*' in ecclesiology. Every local Church manifests all the fullness of the Church of God, because it *is* the Church of God and not just one part of it.[7]

In other words, the entire Church is indivisibly present, *in all her essential elements*, in every particular Church. It is a matter of Catho-

---

While "reunion without absorption" is correct in principle, on a practical level it is worth asking if any of these communities (Old Catholic, Anglican/Episcopalian, Lutheran and Reformed) is sufficiently distinct in its rites, its spirituality, its discipline, and its articulation of revealed truth to justify its remaining a particular Church within the Catholic Church, but outside the Roman Church. Incorporating most (if not all) of these communities into the Roman Church seems logical, given our common cultural milieu and theological patrimony, as well as Rome's remarkable flexibility (since Vatican II) in adapting its rites to particular cultures and circumstances (e.g., the Anglican and Zairean "usages" of the Roman liturgy).

[7] Nicholas Afanassieff, "The Church Which Presides in Love," trans. Katharine Farrer, in *The Primacy of Peter: Essays in Ecclesiology and the Early Church*, ed. John Meyendorff (Crestwood, N.Y.: St. Vladimir's Seminary Press, 1992), 91-143, and here at 109. (First published in English by The Faith Press, Ltd., 1963.)

Cf. St. Peter Damian, *Super Dominus Vobiscum* 5, 6: "The one is in all and the whole in each and every one," "is the whole in all, and the whole in each and every part" (PL 145:235-36); and St. Hilary of Poitiers, *Tractatus in Psalm.* 14.3: "Although the Church is one throughout the world, nevertheless each and every city has its own Church; and the one is in all, regardless of how many there are, because the one exists in the many."

Von Balthasar notes that the Catholic claim to ecclesial totality is practically unintelligible to modern man, whose world "is marked by the scientific approach that, quite legitimately in its own sphere, tries to interpret all phenomena in a horizontal and quantitative manner in order to make them increasingly perspicuous and synthesizable." — *In the Fullness of Faith*, 14.

lic doctrine that one of these essential elements is the episcopate; hence the episcopate must be present in every particular Church. This ecclesiology was reasserted in a 1992 Letter of the Congregation for the Doctrine of the Faith, which cites article 22 of *Lumen Gentium*:

> For each particular Church to be fully Church, that is, the particular presence of the universal Church with all its essential elements, and hence constituted after the model of the universal Church, there must be present in it, as a proper element, the supreme authority of the Church: the episcopal college "together with their head, the Supreme Pontiff, and never apart from him."[8]

Because the Eucharist is the root of ecclesial communion, it is possible to apply what St. Thomas taught concerning the Eucharistic Presence in analogous fashion to the union existing among the particular Churches. Just as, by the principle of "concomitance,"[9] the whole Christ — Body, Blood, Soul and Divinity — is present under each Eucharistic species, so too, by a relationship of "mutual interiority,"[10] the entire Church of Christ — One, Holy, Catholic and Apostolic — is present in every particular Church.

Given that the episcopate in communion with the successor of Peter is divinely instituted and essential to the one Church, which exists in and is formed from the particular Churches,[11] then reunion without hierarchical integration is not possible. The 1992 Letter elsewhere states: "The primacy of the Bishop of Rome and the episcopal college are proper elements of the universal Church" and

---

[8] Congregation for the Doctrine of the Faith, "Letter to the Bishops of the Catholic Church on Some Aspects of the Church Understood As Communion," *Communionis Notio* (May 28, 1992), no. 13.

[9] *Summa Theol.*, III, q. 76, a. 1.

[10] C.D.F., *Communionis Notio*, nn. 9 and 13.

[11] LG 23.

are therefore "interior to each particular Church."[12] Hence there can be no such thing as a non-episcopal particular Church within the universal Church. Even the local parish, which is the "lowest" level of the Church, is "episcopal," in that its presbyters represent the bishop and are the bishop's co-workers for the fulfillment of the Church's apostolic mission.[13] To be the Catholic Church in her fullness, a particular Church requires the episcopate in communion with the Bishop of Rome. A plan to bring the separated communions into organic unity must consider how the sacrament of Order (and therefore the Eucharist) will be introduced or reintroduced to the Churches which lack them. With this in mind, it is time to consider other proposals.

### b. Recognize existing non-Catholic ministries?

Let us begin by taking into account the various objections to the validity of Orders and (most) sacraments in the Reformation communities and their offshoots. One objection is that the Council of Trent denied the validity of Protestant ministries. Not so, Harry McSorley has argued, pointing out that

> Catholic theologians who have maintained that there is no sacrament of the Body and Blood of Christ in Protestant Churches because Protestant ministers are radically incapable of consecrating the Eucharist are incorrect if they think this opinion is necessitated by the teaching of Trent.[14]

Recall that the Council of Trent did not explicitly pronounce Protestant ministries invalid, but simply not "legitimate" inasmuch

---

[12] C.D.F., *Communionis Notio*, no. 13.

[13] PO 2; CCC 1562.

[14] Harry J. McSorley, "Trent and the Question: Can Protestant Ministers Consecrate the Eucharist?" in *Lutherans and Catholics in Dialogue*, vol. 4, *Eucharist and Ministry* (Washington: U.S. Catholic Conference, 1970), 283-99, quote at 299.

as they violated the traditional discipline of the Church. No less an authority than Cardinal Ratzinger would seem to confirm McSorley's position:

> Catholic teaching... does not in any way deny that Protestant Christians who believe in the presence of the Lord also share in that presence.[15]

Viewed from this perspective alone, the question of Order and the Lord's Supper in Reformed Christianity might pertain more to liceity than to validity, as we shall investigate below.

A second objection to the validity of Protestant ministries is that Luther and the other Reformers could not validly ordain, because they themselves were not bishops. Whether simple priests can validly ordain is a question open to debate in Catholic theology.[16] But even granted that such powers were exercised by the priest-abbots in England and Germany (as we saw in Chapter Four), authorization from Rome was necessary for such ordinations to be recognized (rightly or wrongly) as valid: a requisite not necessary where the bishop is the ordainer. Thus in every respect the ministry of a simple priest was dependent upon the local bishop or upon the Roman Pontiff. Furthermore, these papal "dispensations" antedated by more than a century the Council of Trent, which decreed that bishops are the proper and ordinary ministers of the sacrament of Order.[17]

There is yet a third objection to the validity of Protestant ministries. The Reformers deliberately altered the Roman Church's

---

[15] PCT, 236. The context in which this sentence occurs suggests that the author is speaking of a sacramental presence.

[16] As we read in the official *relatio* to LG 21: "The Commission decided that nothing should be declared concerning the question, whether only a bishop can ordain priests and therefore it has settled neither the question of law nor of fact." — *Schema Constitutionis de Ecclesia* (Vatican, 1964), 87.

[17] Attempting to reconcile these dispensations to the teaching of Trent (DS 1768 and 1777), J. Neuner, S.J., and J. Dupuis, S.J., explain that "they can be understood either

ordination rite and its accompanying prayers in order to express their denial of the sacramentality of Order and the powers conferred by it, in particular the power to confect the Eucharist for offering sacrifice. Whether the Reformers could confer Order in extraordinary circumstances is immaterial: their intention *not* to ordain sacrificing priests nullified the general intention to do what the Church does. In the language of sacramental theology, both "form" and "intention" were flawed: defective *form*, because of the deliberate act against the creation of a Eucharistic ministry of consecration and sacrifice ("Massing priests"); and defective *intention*, because of the ambiguity concerning the nature of the ministries of presbyter and bishop. This judgment is usually brought forward in reference to Anglican ordinations.

The English Reformation was carried through in large measure by *bishops*, who themselves were consecrated by bishops who had broken with the Pope under King Henry VIII's *Act of Supremacy* (1534). In the years immediately following the schism, the Church of England remained effectively Catholic in belief and practice, and ordinations were conferred by true bishops in accordance with the rite of the Roman Pontifical. But by 1550 the national Church was more decidedly Protestant, having come under the influence of Lutheranism and (especially) Calvinism. In that year Thomas

---

as 'untying' a radical power conferred by priestly ordination which needs to be untied for its valid exercise, or as an exceptional power granted to priests as extraordinary ministers of the sacrament, in virtue of the Pope's own 'eminent power' (*potestas excellentiæ*) over the sacramental rites and their ministers." — *The Christian Faith in the Doctrinal Documents of the Catholic Church*, 6th rev. ed. (New York: Alba House, 1996), 670.

   Bernard Dupuy, O.P., provides a similar explanation: "The only way to square these facts and these variations in Church discipline is to regard the functions of the priest as a toning down of the bishop's functions. Their power, of itself, is radically identical (*potestas ordinis*), but ordinarily it is bound (*potestas legata*)." — "Is There a Dogmatic Distinction between the Function of Priests and the Function of Bishops?" in *Concilium* 34 (1968): 74-86, at 86.

   Cf. J. Beyer, "Nature et position du Sacerdoce," *Nouvelle Revue Théologique* 76 (1954): 364-76, which regards these papal dispensations as an abuse.

Cranmer, the Protestant-minded Archbishop of Canterbury, in the reign of King Edward VI, set aside the Roman Pontifical for a new ordinal which made no reference to a sacrifical priesthood, prompting Roman doubts about the validity of Orders conferred under this new rite. For over three centuries, Catholic and Anglican theologians debated (with each other and within their own ranks) the validity of Anglican ordinations conferred according to the Edwardine ordinal. To discuss this very complex question at great length would take us too far afield. It suffices to mention that the pronouncement of Pope Leo XIII in his Bull *Apostolicæ Curæ* of 1896,[18] that Anglican Orders are invalid, retains its binding force.[19]

---

[18] DS 3315-19.

[19] Church historian John Jay Hughes (a Catholic priest), arguing in favor of Anglican Orders, wrote: "The elimination of sacrificial references in the Anglican ordinal, which is said to be the basic reason for the invalidity of Anglican Orders, can only be understood against the background of the contemporary Mass system, and of the theology it produced. As children of their age the Reformers could judge the school theology of Eucharistic Sacrifice only in the light of the Masses that were being paid for and celebrated in such vast numbers on every hand, and of the ideas thought up to justify this system." — "Recent Studies of the Validity of Anglican Orders," *Concilium*, vol. 31, *The Sacraments in General: A New Perspectve*, ed. Edward Schillebeeckx and Boniface Willems (New York: Paulist Press, 1968), 135-46, quote at 143. For a contrary view, cf. Francis Clark, S.J., *Eucharistic Sacrifice and the Reformation* (London and Westminster, Md., 1960), who contends that the English Reformers knew full-well the authentic Catholic doctrine of the Eucharist, and it is precisely *that*, not some alleged aberration, which they rejected.

It is also noted that at the time of Leo XIII the *Apostolic tradition* of Hippolytus had not yet been discovered. The ordination rite given by Hippolytus makes no mention of a Eucharistic priesthood and lacks sacrificial vocabulary, prompting Osborne to write (*Priesthood*, 297): "If this lack, either in intention or in form, is the very reason, according to the Leonine document, which nullifies the Anglican Orders, then it must be likewise stated that the presbyteral Orders conferred through the ritual of Hippolytus... should be considered nullified as well. It would seem, however, that no scholar, Roman Catholic or otherwise, would want to do this."

Osborne gives the false impression that *Apostolicæ Curæ* rests its case on the mere absence of sacrificial and sacerdotal language in the Anglican ordinal. In point of fact, Leo XIII's decision stresses the thoroughness with which the English Reformers had eliminated the idea of Eucharistic Sacrifice by the systematic suppression of prayers and rubrics making this doctrine explicit. There is a difference between not speaking of Eucharistic priesthood and Sacrifice (Hippolytus), and deleting such references from an already existing ordinal (Cranmer). It does not follow, therefore, that because St. Hippolytus' ordination ritual is acceptable, so too is the Anglican ordinal of Edward VI.

We have considered the principal objections to the sacramental validity of Protestant ordinations. The first objection, that Trent denied their validity, is not supported by historical facts. Trent did not explicitly reject the validity of Protestant ministries, but declared them illegitimate. The second objection, that the Reformers could not ordain validly because they were not bishops, might be contested on the grounds that simple priests have performed ordinations which were recognized by the Church. However, these exceptional ordinations always had authorization from the bishop or from the Holy See, whereas the ordinations of the Reformers did not. Even if episcopal authorization of these ordinations is required only for liceity and not for validity, there is still a third objection which, unlike the first two, cannot be reasonably challenged: that defective form and intention nullified Protestant ordinations. In view of this, it seems impossible that the Church can recognize the sacramental validity of Protestant office.

### c. "Validate" non-Catholic ministries?

The Catholic Church can supply, modify, or dispense with the form of the sacraments for a good reason. She has done so with Matrimony (canonical form is often dispensed with, or is supplied by *sanatio in radice*) and with Confirmation (the form was revised after Vatican II). Insofar as the Protestant Reformers were convinced that breaking with the papal Church was the only way to reform the whole of Church life according to the Gospel, could the Catholic Church supply for any defects inherent in Protestant ministries? Could the Church "validate" these ministries by evoking the principle of *Ecclesia supplet* ("the Church supplies") or of "economy" in Orthodox terminology?[20]

Methodist theologian Albert Outler proposes that historical circumstances may sometimes validate irregular ordinations such that "at least some of the Protestant ministries might very well be redefined, not as schismatic or heretical, but rather as 'extraordinary'…"[21] The ecumenical task, as Outler sees it, is to find a formula that allows for "regularization" without abjuration.

Whether the Church can supply for sacramental defects in Protestantism depends, at least in part, on the degree to which she can extrapolate the good faith intentions of the Reformers, however one might oppose their doctrinal conclusions. Luther and the other Reformers did not initially intend to establish new Churches, but to bring the Catholic Church into conformity with their understanding of evangelical faith and life. On this basis, some would credit them with acting in good faith. As one Presbyterian theologian explains:

> "The Reformed Church" does not set out to be a new or another Church but to be a movement of reform within the One Holy Catholic and Apostolic Church of Jesus Christ, in obedience to its apostolic foundation in Him, and through constant renewing of the Holy Spirit.… The Reformed Church claims to be both "Apostolic" and "Catholic", for it does not look to any other foundation than that of the Apostolic Church in what it received from Christ and in His one Spirit and handed on to the world through the Holy Scriptures and through a ministry dependent on it. The Reformed Church interprets this apostolic Tradition in agreement with and on the basis of the Catholic theology of the Ecumenical Councils of the undivided Church.[22]

---

[20] Recognition of Anglican Orders by some Orthodox is given by virtue of "economy," a mitigation of the rigorousness (*akribeia*) of the law in view of a greater good. See A. Alivisatos, "'Economy' from the Orthodox Point of View" in *Dispensation in Practice and Theory* (London, 1944), 27.

[21] Albert Outler, "How can we arrive at a Theological and Practical, Mutual Recognition of Ministries? A Methodist Reply," *Concilium* 74 (1972): 83-91, quote at 87.

[22] Thomas F. Torrance, "Memoranda on Orthodox/Reformed Relations," chap. in *Theological Dialogue between Orthodox and Reformed Churches*, ed. Thomas F. Torrance (Edinburgh/London: Scottish Academic Press, 1985), 3.

Even the Catholic historian and apologist Hilaire Belloc, scarcely affirmative of the Reformers themselves, could sympathize with their original aims:

> Only a few of the most bitter or ardent Reformers set out to destroy Catholicism as a separate existing thing of which they were conscious and which they hated. Still less did most of the Reformers set out to erect some other united counter-religion.
>
> They set out (as they themselves put it and as it had been put for a century and a half before the great upheaval) "to reform." They professed to purify the Church and to restore it to its original virtues of directness and simplicity. They professed in their various ways (and the various groups of them differed in almost everything except their increasing reaction against unity) to get rid of excrescences, superstitions and historical falsehoods — of which, Heaven knows, there was a multitude for them to attack.[23]

In the face of the opposition of many bishops to serious Church reform (before Trent), Luther was convinced that reformation had to go on, even if without the support of the hierarchy. "At the same time," Küng believes,

> he altogether hoped that this was only a choice of practical expediency, that it would be temporary, and neither fundamental nor final. He hoped that in time the bishops would renew themselves in the apostolic spirit, that they would return to an apostolic way of life and work, that they would change from wolves into shepherds of Christ's flock: and that in the proclamation of the Gospel and the exercise of pastoral care they would once more turn into true successors of the apostles.[24]

---

[23] Hilaire Belloc, *The Great Heresies* (London: Sheed & Ward, 1938; repr., Rockford, Ill.: TAN Books and Publishers, Inc., 1991), 99.

[24] Küng, *Structures of the Church*, 127-28; cf. *idem*, *The Church*, 247-49.

History has often traced doctrinal disputes to a misunderstanding of terminology, to different conceptual frameworks, or to different emphases of the same truth.[25] These disputes are usually aggravated by historical circumstances and by polemics which generate more heat than light. Owing to the successes of the modern ecumenical movement, many Catholic and Protestant theologians nowadays are of the opinion that the doctrines of grace and justification need no longer divide Christians. Objective differences still remain between the doctrines of the sixteenth-century Reformers and of the Catholic Church: Luther, Calvin and Zwingli plainly depart from the whole of Tradition in their understanding of the sacraments. Still, many theologians and Church historians would agree today that the essence of the Reformation was a misunderstanding. As one former Lutheran pastor who is now a Catholic priest once remarked, the Reformation should have been a blip in the history of Christianity, not a permanent fracture. We need to look at these doctrinal differences in the entire context of a critical investigation of the Reformation if we would extrapolate good faith intentions. It has been suggested that such a reassessment would almost certainly cast a great deal of light on the problems involved in the recognition or regularization of Protestant ministries, but maybe this is pressing the issue too far. While it is true that the contemporary reassessment of the Reformation has cleared up misunderstandings, it is probably too optimistic to expect from this any justification for validating Protestant ordinations. The considered

---

[25] When, for example, in the tempest of the Trinitarian controversies, the work of the Cappodocian Fathers helped to clarify the meaning of the terms *hupostasis* and *ousia*, some theologians who were suspected of heterodoxy were in fact vindicated.

Similarly, Rahner remarks that "much of what provoked the protest of Evangelical Christianity at the time of the Reformation, for example, the doctrine of freedom, the doctrine of merit, and the doctrine of so-called infused grace, could perhaps at the time, and certainly can now, be recognized as a mutual misunderstanding and can be laid to rest." — *Foundations of Christian Faith*, 360.

opinion of theologians, both Catholic and Orthodox, is that the principle of *Ecclesia supplet*, or "economy," is simply not that elastic, and cannot be applied to cases where the episcopal succession has been disrupted.[26]

Admitting or supplying for the validity of ministry and sacraments requires more than the assurance of good faith. It requires the presence of valid ministers of Order, which for Catholicism means bishops within the apostolic succession. Before Protestant ministries can be recognized as "valid," they must be fully and visibly integrated into that classical form of ministry and in that hierarchical descent which is constitutive of Catholic (and Orthodox) ecclesiology. Recognizing or validating ministries is not the first but the *final* stage in bringing about reunion. Russian Orthodox theologian Fr. Boris Bobrinskoy points out some of the many issues to consider before proceeding with a mutual recognition of ministries, or indeed before adopting any proposal to implement corporate reintegration:

> To "recognize" the ordained minister of a Church is necessarily to recognize its faith, doctrine, teaching, living witness of sanctity and love, and not merely the "validity" of an ordination or the historically continuous nature of a succession.

> "Recognition" of the ministry therefore has to be a total and full recognition in a reciprocal creative tension of faith and life, of truth and sanctity, of the sacramental structures and the grace which grounds and gives them life....[27]

---

[26] Miguel M. Garijo-Guembe, *Communion of the Saints: Foundation, Nature, and Structure of the Church*, trans. Patrick Madigan, S.J. (Collegeville, Mn.: Liturgical Press, 1994), 192-93 (with bibliography). (Original German: *Gemeinschaft der Heiligen: Grund, Wesen und Struktur der Kirche* [Patmos Verlag GmbH, 1988].)

[27] Boris Bobrinskoy, "How can we arrive at a Theological and Practical, Mutual Recognition of Ministries? An Orthodox Reply," *Concilium* 74 (1972): 63-75, quote at 70.

### d. Joint ordinations?

Still another strategy for restoring visible communion involves holding joint ordinations. The Catholic Church and the separated community in question would of course first make publicly known their full consensus in matters of faith, such that all that remains for the restoration of full ecclesial unity is the reestablishment of hierarchical communion. In other words, for all practical purposes, the "separated" communion is separated only juridically, and is now prepared for reintegration into the Catholic Church through juridical and sacramental communion within the Church's apostolic succession of bishops. Under this scheme, Catholic bishops and non-Catholic ministers would participate in each other's ordinations. Over time, the ordained ministers of the "reunited" Church would be the progeny of the formerly separated Churches.

Of course, this proposal poses little problem when it comes to joint ordinations involving those whose Orders the Catholic Church already recognizes as valid, such as the Orthodox and Old Catholic bishops. But one can anticipate white-hot controversy when it comes to joint ordinations involving the clergy of the non-episcopal ecclesial communities. In these instances it will have to be emphasized that defective (heretical) intention is not an issue anymore: these ministers have accepted the full Catholic doctrine regarding the sacrament of Order. As long as a Catholic bishop is involved in each ordination, there is assurance of sacramental validity (provided of course that *his* intention is orthodox). As the years pass and the scars of separation fade, all the clergy in the "reunited" Church will be episcopally ordained, and the question of whose Orders are valid and whose are invalid will be moot.

This strategy, if controversial, is not unprecedented. A similar plan was put into practice in the formation in 1948 of the Church of South India, the amalgamation of an episcopal Church with

others whose tradition was non-episcopal. Anglicans, Congrega-
tionalists, Methodists and Presbyterians in southern India united
to form one Church. Jesuit theologian Fr. Bernard Leeming de-
scribes the strategy laid down in the Church's "Constitution" of
1952:

> All ordinations after the union are to be by an imposition
> of hands by bishops, with presbyters also laying on hands.
> Thus in the course of time, all the ministers will be episco-
> pally ordained. Meantime, there are ministers episcopally
> ordained before the union [the Anglicans], those never epis-
> copally ordained [the Protestants of various kinds], and
> those episcopally ordained after the union. The difference
> between the two classes of episcopally ordained ministers
> is that no Anglican would doubt the Orders conferred be-
> fore the union, whereas some have questioned the Orders
> conferred after the union, on grounds of ambiguity of faith
> and "intention."[28]

Of course, problems abounded. Leeming mentions difficulties arising in the Church of England about admitting the Church
of South India into communion. Attention focused on the validity
of the ordinations, when neither the ordained nor the ordainer nor,
in fact, the whole body of the Church might have right faith about
the Eucharist and the episcopacy. Here we see the importance of
complete concordance in faith before attempting such an enterprise.
The unhappy experiences of the Church of South India have made
it clear that it is not enough simply to mingle existing ministries
without some definite visible act of unification. This leads to strains
within the new united Church.

---

[28] Bernard Leeming, S.J., *The Churches and the Church: A Study of Ecumenism* (London:
Darton, Longman & Todd; Westminster, Md.: The Newman Press, 1960), 13.

*Summary*

We have considered various proposals for assimilating non-Catholic ministries outside the apostolic succession: (a) permit non-episcopal congregations to exist within the unity of the Catholic Church; (b) recognize non-Catholic ministries as valid, but illicit; (c) somehow "validate" non-Catholic ministries by applying the principle of *Ecclesia supplet*; and (d) have joint ordinations.

Catholic ecclesiology does not authorize proposal (a), given that the Church is wholly present in the particular Churches, and that the episcopacy is essential to Church's constitution. Proposals (b) and (c) seem very problematic: for even if there were no defect of form, there certainly was defect of intention (Protestantism rejects the sacramentality of Order and the sacrificial character of the Eucharist), and the principle of *Ecclesia supplet* can go only so far. Proposal (d) arguably merits further investigation.

### 8.2. *Preserving the integrity of Order in the future*

"The best contribution we can make to ecumenical understanding," Bishop Kasper believes, "is to emphasize the interdependence of *traditio, successio* and *communio* ourselves, not only in theory, but first and foremost in Church practice."[29] What concrete measures could the Catholic Church take to meet this challenge?

It has been amply demonstrated that the authentic apostolic succession has a "triune" character, consisting of three deeply interrelated aspects: (1) the unbroken genealogy of apostolic office, (2) fidelity to the apostolic teaching, and (3) catholicity, that is, life in the communion of the Churches, manifest by the collegiality of bishops under the leadership of the Roman Pontiff. Thus it would

---

[29] Kasper, 15-16.

seem well to agree with Cyprian to some measure: schism *per se* incurs the loss of the apostolic succession and of (most) valid sacraments. Still, we would not want to disregard the strength of Augustine's position: all sacraments, even those administered in schism, derive their efficacy wholly from Christ and not in any way from the ordained themselves. Certain medieval theologians recognized the need somehow to balance the Augustinian and Cyprianic sub-traditions, allowing them to modify each other.[30]

Applying this recommendation to our own day, the Catholic Church could follow Augustine in affirming the retention of the apostolic succession (and hence a valid sacramental ministry) in those episcopal Churches which have broken communion with the Roman Church, while following Cyprian in denying that this process is indefinitely extensible. In effect, "the Augustinian principle operates for one sacramental generation, after which the Cyprianic principle takes over."[31] The Catholic Church would recognize the Orders of schismatic bishops who had been ordained as Catholics, but would not recognize the ordinations conferred by them in schism. A bishop who breaks communion with the Catholic Church, who establishes another *communio* and hence another Church, would lose the ability to pass on the apostolic priesthood.

On the surface, this proposal seems flawed and contradictory. Surely, it is incongruous to argue that a bishop cannot validly (albeit illicitly) confer Orders after going into schism? After all, the act of schism does not strip him of the fullness of Order, and therefore of his power to ordain. The Catholic Church recognizes the separated Eastern communions as Churches (and not simply as "ecclesial communities") precisely because these Churches have

---

[30] Nichols, 59.

[31] *Ibid.*, 68-69. Among the early medieval scholars who held this intermediate position were the German theologian Bernold of Constance (ca. 1054-1100) and St. Bruno of Segni (1049-1123), the theological adviser of Pope Bl. Urban II.

bishops whose origins in the apostolic succession are unquestioned.[32] So the matter would seem closed.

But the problem is more complex than that. The mere fact that one is a bishop does not guarantee his ability to ordain validly. To recall the teaching of the Council of Florence, proper matter and form, together with the proper minister's intention to "do what the Church does," are required for the validity of any sacrament.[33] Therefore, the proposal to withhold the recognition of ordinations conferred by a schismatic bishop is not inherently flawed; his intention must always be taken into account.

Having said that, let us now consider whether the Church, exercising her authority to bind and to loose (Mt 16:19),[34] could reasonably include *full ecclesial communion* as a prerequisite for sacramental validity. Vorgrimler writes:

> According to Catholic belief, it is the Church's task to recognize the necessary conditions for the validity and liceity of a sacramental action and to establish appropriate norms. Since the sacraments are the Church's liturgy, there is no doubt that the Church has charge over the design, ordering, and reform of sacramental liturgy.[35]

What we say of Christ, we can say of His Church-Body (and of His Eucharistic Body): she is the great mystery (*sacramentum*), at once visible and invisible, divine and human,[36] which contains and vitalizes all the other sacraments. Like all the sacraments, Order is conferred *by* the Church and *for* the Church.[37] There is no ques-

---

[32] Cf. Sullivan, *The Church We Believe In*, 50-52; also Garijo-Guembe, 193.

[33] DS 1312.

[34] Cf. CCC 553.

[35] Vorgrimler, 91.

[36] Cf. St. Bernard, *Sermo I: De Circumcisione* 2: "The human joins to the divine, the lowest to the highest" (PL 183, 133c).

[37] Cf. CCC 1118.

tion that ecclesial communion is the context for the apostolic succession. The Church's understanding of the deposit of faith, and of her own nature as the fundamental sacrament of Christ, has developed and deepened over the course of twenty centuries of theological reflection.

If, as Vorgrimler has noted, the Church has the authority to "establish appropriate norms" for sacramental validity and liceity, then her adjudication of the validity or invalidity of Order (and hence of the presence of a real succession in the apostolic ministry) should reflect the theological development that has taken place in ecclesiology with regard to the Church's sacramental nature. It seems fitting, therefore, that the Church should adopt a policy of "non-recognition." Accordingly, the classic distinction between sacramental validity and liceity would not apply to those instances when one attempts to confer ordination outside the communion of the "root" sacrament, the Church: the bishop who parts company with the episcopal college ordains invalidly and not merely illicitly.[38]

Two further objections to the proposal of "non-recognition" arise, both of which call attention to an apparent double standard. First, if the Church were no longer to recognize schismatic ordinations, why should she continue to recognize other sacraments celebrated outside full communion? Why apply the Cyprianic principle to Order (and the sacraments dependent upon Order), but the Augustinian principle to Baptism and Matrimony? Secondly, presuming that this policy of "non-recognition" would not be retroactive, but would apply only to those bishops who fall into schism after some future date, then is it not ludicrous to recognize the validity of schismatic ordinations before a certain time, but not af-

---

[38] Karl Rahner, "Über den Episkopat," *Stimmen der Zeit* 173 (1963): 187, claims that sacramental theology is uncertain about the Church's power to deprive an illicit ordination of its validity.

ter? Why deem the ordinations conferred by a future schismatic bishop to be invalid, yet continue to recognize the validity of ordinations conferred in, for instance, the Orthodox Church?

The first objection — that it is discrepant to apply the Cyprianic principle to some sacraments and not to others — overlooks the distinct purposes of each sacrament. Baptism, Matrimony and Order all perpetuate the Church's life, each in its own way. Baptism makes the Christian a cell of that very Body which is Christ's. Matrimony unites Christians to collaborate with God in generating others who will share in the supernatural life. Holy Order configures the Christian to Christ, the only true Priest, even more intimately than Baptism, that he might be a steward of God's mysteries (1 Cor 4:1), making present that Sacrament which is the culmination of the Church's sacramental activity: the Eucharist.[39] It is in the Eucharistic *anamnêsis* of Christ's sacrifice, in which the Church is most intimately joined with Him in Holy Communion, that she *is* most perfectly the Church. "This is to say unequivocally that the other sacraments are also activities *in the Church*, in which her members are prepared in some way for the Eucharist. And since the Eucharist fulfills the perfection of charity in the Church, we may say that in a sense, it commands the other ecclesial actions, just as charity commands all the other virtues of the Christian life."[40] Baptism and Matrimony, it is true can be validly received outside the full communion of the Catholic Church, though they (like all the sacraments) exercise a dynamism ordered toward full communion with Christ and His members — a communion perfectly realized and expressed in the Eucharist. But Order, which was instituted specifically for the sake of making present the great Sacra-

---

[39] St. Thomas, *Summa Theol.*, II, 1. 65, a. 3: "All the other sacraments seem to be ordered to [the Eucharist] as to their end.".

[40] Maurice Bonaventure Schepers, O.P., *The Church of Christ*. Foundations of Catholic Theology Series, ed. Gerard S. Sloyan (Englewood Cliffs, N.J.: Prentice-Hall, Inc., 1963), 92.

ment of communion, demands by its very nature that it reside within the catholic unity of the Church, which is to say the Catholic Church.

Now to address the second objection to our "non-recognition" proposal: that it would be arbitrary to recognize the apostolic succession of bishops in extant non-Catholic Churches, but not in those congregations which, at some time after this proposal goes into effect, commit schism through unauthorized episcopal ordinations. It has already been noted that the Church possesses authority to establish requirements for sacramental validity. The conditions which give validity or efficacy to a particular sacramental celebration today — its words, gestures, and other circumstances — can change, such that what is "valid" under present-day norms might not be valid under future norms.

For instance, the requirements for a valid marriage have changed over the centuries. In addition to the absolute proscriptions of the natural law and of the Commandments, the Church herself has established certain impediments (restrictions) to marriage, which she can dispense or lift in certain cases (for example, marriage between a Catholic and a baptized non-Catholic). Moreover, it was not until the Council of Trent that Latin-rite Catholics were obliged to marry in the presence of a priest and witnesses. (This requirement, of course, did not nullify all previous marriages which did not follow this form.) For the validity of the sacrament of Matrimony, it is necessary that the spouses, at the time they exchange consent, intend to enter into a permanent and monogamous union that is open to the procreation and rearing of children. If a man and a woman marry with the intention of not having children, thereby violating one of the purposes and goods of marriage, they contract marriage invalidly (that is, they do not receive the sacrament of Matrimony), because they lack the intention of receiving the sacrament.

Returning to the question of ordination, full communion in the Catholic Church could be made a criterion for the validity of Order in the future, perhaps coming under the rubric of proper intention.[41] By ordaining bishops, the Church intends to perpetuate sacramentally the apostolic succession, which is not so much personal as *collegial*: the succession of apostolic ministry is perpetuated by the college of bishops collectively, under the headship of St. Peter's successor. To ordain without a papal mandate incurs automatic excommunication[42] and at least *connotes* a schismatic intention.[43] Does a bishop who ordains illicitly, with the intention

---

[41] Bernard Leeming, "Are They Really Bishops?" *Heythrop Journal* 5 (1964): 259-67, raises the question whether proper intention exists, or even can exist, on the part of a bishop who attempts to ordain against the will of the episcopal college.

[42] *Codex Iuris Canonici* [Code of Canon Law], can. 1382.

[43] Church law distinguishes between excommunication and schism. Canon 751 defines schism as "the refusal of submission to the Roman Pontiff or of communion with members of the Church subject to him." "The act of consecrating a bishop (without a papal mandate) is not *in itself* a schismatic act," said R. Castillo Cardinal Lara, head of the Pontifical Commission for the Authentic Interpretation of Legislative Texts, shortly after the illicit consecrations of June 30, 1988, carried out by French Archbishop Marcel Lefebvre, founder of the Society of St. Pius X (SSPX). "In fact," Lara continued, "the code that deals with offenses is divided into two sections. One deals with offenses against religion and the unity of the Church, and these are apostasy, schism, and heresy. Consecrating a bishop without a pontifical mandate is, on the contrary, an offense against the exercise of a specific ministry. For example, in the case of the consecrations carried out by the Vietnamese Archbishop Ngo Dinh Thuc in 1976 and 1983, although the archbishop was excommunicated he was not considered to have committed a schismatic act because there was no intention of a breach with the Church"; quoted in Roger McCaffrey, "What Does the Vatican Now Consider 'Schismatic'? *The Latin Mass* (Sept.-Oct. 1993): 4.

Pope John Paul II obviously saw things differentlyd when he stated with regard to Lefebvre: "In itself, this act was one of disobedience to the Roman Pontiff in a very grave matter and of supreme importance for the unity of the Church, such as is the ordination of bishops whereby the apostolic succession is sacramentally perpetuated. Hence such disobedience — which implies in practice the rejection of the Roman primacy — constitutes a schismatic act"; apostolic letter *Ecclesia Dei* (July 2, 1988). On the one hand, John Paul II is not a canonist, but a philosopher and theologian; on the other hand, as Pope he is the Church's supreme legislator.

Yet even if canonically Lefebvre's ordinations did not amount to schism, the SSPX's refusal of unambiguous communion with Rome surely gives evidence of a schismatic posture. This excerpt from an article in the SSPX English-language monthly is typical of the rhetoric of SSPX apologists: "A mere act of disobedience to a superior does not imply denial that the superior holds office or has authority.... [F]or the charge of

of setting up a "parallel" Church apart from the episcopal college, really intend to continue the *true* apostolic succession?

Having addressed a few of the imaginable objections to the proposed "non-recognition" policy, it is necessary at this point to explain what the terms "validity" and "invalidity" would mean under our proposal. The Holy Spirit is at work in the Church; for He is her Artisan and Source of her supernatural life, and she is His temple. On the basis of His own freedom, He binds Himself to word and sacrament to reveal His power. "Validity," then would mean what it has always meant, namely: that the efficacy of the Church's sacraments — the sacramental grace — is *assured* by faith and the gift of the Spirit. But the Spirit of God, if domiciled in the Church, is not domesticated in her. God's saving grace is not totally dependent on the sacraments, nor — and here we uphold St. Augustine — is it restricted to the visible limits of the Church. We cannot say where the Spirit is not working, for He blows where He will (Jn 3:8); and "where God's Spirit is, there is the Church and every grace."[44] Thus, "invalidity" would *not* mean that a schismatic bishop's ordinations, and the sacraments which depend on valid Order, are undoubtedly null and devoid of objective sacramental reality; rather, it would mean that *assurance* of their efficacy cannot be posited, and therefore they cannot be relied upon.

Ordination is an action through which the Church realizes her being; it is in this sense that Order is truly a sacrament. The validity of the sacraments is tied up with the activity of the whole

<hr />

'schism' to stick, it must be certain beyond all reasonable doubt. Traditional Catholics have merely remained faithful to what the Church has always taught and done, and this fidelity to tradition is the sole cause of all their problems with authority.... It is now for the Pope and those who claim to be 'faithful' to him to explain their actions, and to show that they are still Catholics. The six bishops involved in the events of 30th June have made their orthodoxy clear"; Fr. T.C.G. Glover, "Schism and Monsignor Lefebvre," *The Angelus* (August 1992): 22-23.

[44] St. Irenaeus, *Adv. Hær.* 3.24.1; PG 7, 966.

Church, not with a sacramental act taken in isolation. Every individual act of sacramental ordination is therefore an expression of the continuing apostolicity and Catholicity of the whole Church.

Alas, we find ourselves having come full-circle to the point made at the outset of this book, namely, that the key to further progress in Christian unity lies in that most basic question: *What is meant by "the Church"?* Catholic, Orthodox, Anglican, Lutheran and Reformed Christians alike can agree in principle that the true apostolic ministry is found solely in the Church of Christ. Yet each of these Christian communions understands the mystery of the Church more or less differently from the others. Any Christian denomination that acknowledges catholicity as a mark of the true Church from earliest times — as the ancient creeds attest — naturally will identify itself in some way with the one "catholic Church." The mainline Protestant bodies see themselves as the "reform movement" within the catholic Church. The Anglican Church claims to be a branch of the catholic Church, alongside the Roman and Eastern Churches. The Orthodox Church makes the absolute claim of being the catholic Church. The "Catholic Church" — that communion of distinct Churches which are united to the Church of Rome — considers herself to be the true and essential form of Christianity, the fullest embodiment of the catholic Church (while acknowledging elements of the Church outside her visible, canonical communion).

If non-Catholic Christians are in real, though imperfect, communion with the one Church, the "Catholic Church," are there "degrees" of apostolic succession (correlative to the "degree" of catholicity found in a given communion)? If so, what does this mean? On the one hand, to speak of sacramental validity in degrees is senseless: a man cannot be partially ordained any more than the Eucharist can be partially consecrated or Confirmation partially bestowed. On the other hand, to rest content with the conventional distinction between "material" and "formal" succession — the latter including the legitimate exercise of jurisdictional power — then the problem of Order divorced from communion (what we have been calling "apocryphal" succession) will proliferate unchecked. Schism has always bred schism, and always will. From ancient times, the Church has grappled with the problem of "rival altars" set up by illegitimate ordinations. At least in the Latin West, which sanctioned Augustine's position rather than Cyprian's, most of these ordinations are deemed "valid" by conventional standards. It is in the best interest of all the Churches to make progress toward that day when there will no longer be recognition of the apostolic priesthood outside the one household of apostolic faith — a household as visible as a city set on a hill.

Regrettably, though, it seems that there will always be divisions, and it is simply unrealistic to expect this policy of "non-recognition" to be deferred until that time when all Christian bodies live in Catholic unity. Never has a group which has broken communion with the Roman Pontiff ever admitted to breaking with "*the* Church." Nor should one expect a future schismatic group to do so, if history has taught us anything. However much the separated Churches and sects might disagree theologically with one another, all share the conviction that Rome has erred somewhere along the way, that she has departed from the true faith, and hence from the true Church. Protestantism charges Rome with perverting the apostolic faith and encumbering it with the false gospel of human tradition; Orthodoxy accuses Rome of arrogating to herself an authority not accorded her in apostolic and early patristic times;[45] while separated "traditionalist" groups (some of which are

---

[45] Harmonizing with the Orthodox view is the Old Catholic Church, a loose communion of autonomous episcopates formed by German, Austrian and Swiss Catholics who rejected the dogma of Papal Infallibility as defined in Vatican Council I. Episcopal succession was established in 1874 with the ordination of a German Old Catholic

sedevacantist) denounce "Modern Rome" for breaking with Tradition.[46] Resounding through the ages are the voices of Novatian
in the third century and Donatus in the fourth, joining those of
Wyclif in the fourteenth, Luther and Calvin in the sixteenth,
Dölinger in the nineteenth, Feeney and Lefebvre in the twentieth.
Each sounds his own protest, desiring to safeguard the true deposit
of faith, or some portion of it, from a real or perceived threat; but
if, in his attempt to protect it, he distorts it or he fails to see the
totality of revelation, then he sounds a note that is either discor-
dant or too loud, and he spoils the magnificent symphony of Tradition. There is harmony among the dissenters only where certain
doctrines are held in common; and the refrain thunders: "The Pope
is wrong; Tradition is with *us!*"

Having been keenly aware of the sophistries of the human
intellect after man's fall from grace, the Incarnate Word saw fit to
found His Church upon the rock of the Apostle Peter, so that, after all parties have voiced their beliefs, ultimately one man might
pronounce with one voice the faith of the one Church.[47] The great

---

bishop by a prelate of the Church of Utrecht, which itself severed relations with Rome
in 1724. According to the Declaration of Utrecht (1889), Old Catholics accept the
decrees of the first eight ecumenical councils, but, largely due to Protestant influences,
reject certain distinctively Roman Catholic doctrines and practices. The Bishop of
Rome is recognized as having merely a primacy of honor, but not a primacy of
jurisdiction or infallibility.

[46] Quite telling is the following statement, made by theologians who supported
Archbishop Lefebvre's illicit episcopal ordinations of June 30, 1988: "Schism means a
rupture, a break with the Church and its head, the Pope. (This is, of course, when the
Pope is with the Church.) [The saying "*Ubi Petrus, ibi Ecclesia* — Where is Peter, there
is the Church," is true, but does not mean that one should follow the Pope where he
errs!...] On the other hand, to break with those who have broken with Tradition is not
schism, but fidelity! [only inasmuch as they have broken with Tradition; not to break
with them inasmuch as they are the successor of St. Peter.]" — *The Angelus* (July 1988):
43. (The bracketed text appears in the editor's notes at the bottom of the page.)

[47] "How fortunate you must be to be able to appeal to the Pope; appeal to the Lutheran
synods merely leads to greater disunity." — Lutheran theologian Rudolf Bultmann,
writing to Karl Rahner; cited in Stanley L. Jaki, *And On This Rock*, rev. ed. (Manassas,
Va.: Trinity Communications, 1987), 121.

symphony of Tradition has a conductor, and his name is Peter.[48] To him fell the awesome ministry of binding, loosing, compelling, teaching and confirming the other leaders of the Church. Tradition must be concentrated and personified in Peter's successors, the bishops of Rome, while at the same time not overstating their authority; otherwise, there can be no final resolution of conflicts in the Church.[49] In that famous paraphrase of St. Augustine, "*Roma locuta, causa finita* — Rome has spoken, the matter is closed."[50]

Who better than the successor of St. Peter, the head of the apostolic college, to determine where the apostolic succession is, and where it is not? With all ecumenical regard, it is naive to put off enacting the "non-recognition" proposal until that day when every Christian worships in communion with Peter's successor, for this may not happen until the Savior returns to foreclose on human history. At any rate, "Peter" has no less authority in this matter today than he had at the close of the first century, when he reminded the dissident Christians at Corinth who their rightful overseers were.

---

[48] Cf. St. John Chrysostom, *Hom. in illud 'Hoc scitote'* 4: Peter is "the coryphaeus of the choir, the mouthpiece of the apostolic company, the head of that band, the leader of the whole world, the foundation of the Church, the ardent lover of Christ"; in Kelly, 408.

[49] Cf. George William Rutler, "What is Rome?" *Homiletic & Pastoral Review* (May 1992): 8-15, but esp. 13-14. Two fine apologetical treatments of Petrine primacy from unusual perspectives are Stanley L. Jaki's *And on This Rock*, rev. ed. (Manassas, Va.: Trinity Communications, 1987), and *The Keys of the Kingdom: A Tool's Witness to Truth* (Chicago: Franciscan Herald Press, 1986).

[50] *Sermo* 131.6.10; cf. *Contra duas epp. pel.* 2.3.5.

# Epilogue

*"That they may all be one; even as Thou, Father, art in Me,*
*and I in Thee, that they also may be in Us,*
*so that the world may believe that Thou hast sent Me."*

— High-Priestly Prayer of our Lord Jesus Christ (Jn 17:21)

Since the beginning of the ecumenical movement early in the twentieth century, the Churches of a fragmented Christianity have made real progress toward reconciliation. In many of the questions which have divided Christians for centuries, convergence and even mutual consensus have been reached. Full reunion, however, is impeded particularly by unresolved questions of office and ministry in the Church.

To discuss our understanding of the Church's significance, says Bishop Kasper, is the most important unfinished task in ecumenical dialogue. The fundamental question about the Church's nature or *essence* becomes more critical if the separated Churches are to realize the unity for which our Redeemer prayed. Essence divorced from *form*, however, is something either formless or insubstantial and therefore unreal. The Church's essence is always to be found (though not exhaustively) in her historical form:[1] hence one can express the basic ecclesiological question in terms of Tradition and the apostolic succession, as Cardinal Ratzinger has done.

---

[1] Küng, *The Church*, 5-6.

137

Studying the Church in the apostolic and patristic periods, one becomes aware of the reciprocal rapports of the three components of apostolicity: (1) the historic succession, through the sacrament of Order, from the apostles; (2) agreement with the doctrine of the apostles; and (3) communion among the members of the episcopal college. When these essentials are not held together in balance, when one veers to the "left" or to the "right" of a proper understanding of them, as we have seen, the integrity of the Gospel is compromised. Uprooting the biblical word from Tradition — which includes its official guardians — truncates and discredits the Gospel. Wrenching the historic succession of office from communion-in-the-Tradition spawns "apocryphal" succession, the irregularity of Order and sacraments outside the Church's visible unity.

Applying a more critical historical analysis, Catholic and Protestant theologians have come to understand and appreciate the complex reasons underlying each side's doctrinal emphases and methodologies. Consequently, no Catholic spokesperson today would hold that there is an authentic Christian exercise of office where the latter is not supported by the life of the office-bearer. The "mainline" Protestant, on the other hand, can agree that there is apostolicity, in the full sense of that word, only where ministry is rooted in the apostolic succession of pastoral office. In short, a Church cannot be apostolic in its Order and not in its faith, or vice-versa.

What remains is for the Churches to put this balanced, Catholic (in both the generic and the denominational senses of the word) understanding of apostolicity into practice. This means that the Reformation Churches should reinsert themselves into the historical apostolic succession. For the Catholic Church, it means that the time has come to regard "apocryphal" succession as no real succession at all.

A final word. Lest we be tempted to despair, thinking that the reconciliation of Christians to full visible communion is impossible, we are reminded that "Christianity, as a whole, rests on the victory of the improbable, on the impulse of the Holy Spirit."[2] To paraphrase the closing words of Vatican II's "Decree on Ecumenism," Christians must place their hope not so much in theological dexterity as in the love of the Father for the world, in the prayer of the Son for His Church, and in the reconciling power of Their Holy Spirit.

> *"And hope does not disappoint us, because*
> *God's love has been poured into our hearts through the*
> *Holy Spirit Who has been given to us."*
>
> — St. Paul the Apostle, to the Church at Rome (5:5)

# Selected Bibliography

Afanassieff, Nicholas. "The Church Which Presides in Love"
    translated by Katharine Farrer, in *The Primacy of Peter:
    Essays in Ecclesiology and the Early Church*, ed. John
    Meyendorff, 91-143. Crestwood, NY: St. Vladimir's
    Seminary Press, 1992.

Anglican/Roman Catholic International Commission. "Ministry
    and Ordination." In *The Final Report*. Cincinnati: Forward
    Movement Publications; Washington: U.S. Catholic
    Conference, 1982.

Bobrinskoy, Boris. "How can we arrive at a Theological and
    Practical, Mutual Recognition of Ministries? An Orthodox
    Reply." *Concilium*, Vol. 74, *The Plurality of Ministries*, ed.
    Hans Küng and Walter Kasper. New York: Herder &
    Herder, 1972.

Bouyer, Louis. *Dictionary of Theology*. Translated by Charles
    Underhill Quinn. Tournai: Desclée, 1965. S.v. "Protes-
    tants."

_____. *The Church of God*. Translated by Charles Underhill
    Quinn. Chicago: Franciscan Herald Press, 1982.

Brown, Raymond E., S.S. *Priest and Bishop: Biblical Reflections.* New
    York: Paulist Press, 1970.

_____. *The Churches the Apostles Left Behind.* New York:
    Paulist Press, 1984.

*Catechism of the Catholic Church.* Ignatius Press — Libreria Editrice
    Vaticana, 1994.

Clark, Francis, S.J. *Eucharistic Sacrifice and the Reformation.* London
    and Westminster, MD, 1960.

Clarkson, John F., S.J., et al., eds. *The Church Teaches: Documents of the Church in English Translation*. B. Herder Book Co., 1955; reprint, Rockford, IL: TAN Books and Publishers, 1973.

Congar, Yves, O.P. *Chrétiens désunis*. Paris, 1937. English translation: *Divided Christendom*. London, 1939.

Congregation for the Doctrine of the Faith. "Letter to the Bishops of the Catholic Church on Some Aspects of the Church Understood As Communion," *Communionis Notio*, May 28, 1992.

_____. "Declaration in Defense of the Catholic Doctrine of the Church against Certain Errors of the Day," *Mysterium Ecclesiæ*, June 24, 1973.

De Lubac, Henri, S.J. *The Splendor of the Church*. Translated by Michael Mason. New York: Sheed & Ward, 1956; reprint, San Francisco: Ignatius Press, 1986.

Denzinger, Henricus and Adolfus Schönmetzer, S.J. *Enchiridion Symbolorum, definitionum et declarationum de rebus fidei et morum*. 34th ed. Barcelona: Herder, 1967.

Dix, Gregory, O.S.B., ed. *The Treatise on the Apostolic Tradition of Hippolytus of Rome*. London: S.P.C.K., 1937.

Dupuy, Bernard, O.P. "Is There a Dogmatic Distinction between the Function of Priests and the Function of Bishops?" *Concilium*. Vol. 34, *Apostolic Succession: Rethinking a Barrier to Unity*, ed. Hans Küng. New York: Paulist Press, 1968.

Ehrhardt, Arnold. *The Apostolic Succession in the First Two Centuries of the Church*. London: Lutterworth Press, 1953.

Flannery, Austin, O.P., gen. ed. *Vatican Council II. The Conciliar and Post Conciliar Documents*. Rev. ed. Vatican Collection Series. Northport, NY: Costello Publishing Company, 1988.

Garijo-Guembe, Miguel M. *Communion of the Saints: Foundation, Nature and Structure of the Church*. Translated by Patrick Madigan, S.J. Collegeville, MN: Liturgical Press, 1994.

German Bishops' Conference. *The Church's Confession of Faith: A Catholic Catechism for Adults*. Edited by Mark Jordan.

Translated by Stephen Wentworth Arndt. San Francisco: Ignatius Press, 1987 and 1989.

*Growth in Agreement. Reports and Agreed Statements of Ecumenical Conversations at World Level.* Edited by Harding Meyer and Lukas Vischer. New York: Paulist Press; Geneva: WCC, 1984.

Hughes, John Jay. "Recent Studies of the Validity of Anglican Orders." *Concilium.* Vol. 31, *The Sacraments in General: A New Perspective,* ed. Edward Schillebeeckx and Boniface Willems. New York: Paulist Press, 1968.

Javierre, Antonio, S.D.B. *Apostolic Succession: Rethinking a Barrier to Christian Unity.* Glen Rock, NJ: Paulist Press, 1968.

John Paul II, Pope. Encyclical "On Commitment to Ecumenism," *Ut Unum Sint,* May 25, 1995.

Kasper, Walter. Lecture, *Apostolic Succession in Episcopacy in an Ecumenical Context.* Baltimore: St. Mary's Seminary & University, 1992.

Kilmartin, Edward J., S.J. "A Catholic Response to Lima 1982." *One in Christ* 21 (1985): 212-16.

Küng, Hans. *The Church.* Translated by Ray and Rosaleen Ockenden. New York: Sheed & Ward, 1967.

_____. *Structures of the Church.* Translated by Salvator Attanasio. New York: Thomas Nelson & Sons, 1964.

Leeming, Bernard, S.J. "Are They Really Bishops?" *Heythrop Journal* 5, (1964): 259-67.

_____. *The Churches and the Church: A Study of Ecumenism.* London: Darton, Longman & Todd; Westminster, MD: The Newman Press, 1960.

McSorley, Harry J. "Trent and the Question: Can Protestant Ministers Consecrate the Eucharist?" In *Lutherans and Catholics in Dialogue.* Vol. 4, *Eucharist and Ministry.* Washington: U.S. Catholic Conference, 1970.

Meyendorff, John. *Catholicity and the Church.* Crestwood, NY: St. Vladimir's Seminary Press, 1983.

Migne, J.P., ed. *Patrologia Græca.* 162 vols. Paris, 1857 ff.

_____. *Patrologia Latina*. 217 vols. + 4 index vols. Paris, 1844 ff.

Miller, J. Michael, C.S.B. *The Shepherd and the Rock: Origins, Development, and Mission of the Papacy*. Huntington, IN: Our Sunday Visitor, Inc., 1995.

Neuner, J., S.J. and J. Dupuis, S.J., eds. *The Christian Faith in the Doctrinal Documents of the Catholic Church*. 5th rev. ed. New York: Alba House, 1990; 6th rev. ed., 1996.

*New Standard Jewish Encyclopedia*, 1970 ed. S.v. "Ordination."

Newman, John Henry. *The Works of Cardinal Newman*. Vol. 5, *Certain Difficulties Felt by Anglicans in Catholic Teaching*. 2 vols. Westminster, MD: Christian Classics, 1969.

Nichols, Aidan, O.P. *Holy Order: The Apostolic Ministry from the New Testament to the Second Vatican Council*. Oscott Series, gen. eds. Maurice Couve de Murville (Abp. of Birmingham), Frs. David McLoughlin and David Evans, no. 5. Dublin: Veritas, 1990.

Osborne, Kenan B., O.F.M. *Priesthood: A History of the Ordained Ministry in the Roman Catholic Church*. New York: Paulist Press, 1988.

Outler, Albert. "How can we arrive at a Theological and Practical, Mutual Recognition of Ministries? A Methodist Reply." *Concilium*. Vol. 74, *The Plurality of Ministries*, ed. Hans Küng and Walter Kasper. New York: Herder & Herder, 1972.

Quanbeck, Warren A. "A Contemporary View of Apostolic Succession." In *Lutherans and Catholics in Dialogue*. Vol. 4, *Eucharist and Ministry*. Washington: U.S. Catholic Conference, 1970.

Quasten, Johannes, ed. *Patrology*. 3 vols. Utrecht: Spectrum, 1950; reprint, Westminster, MD: Christian Classics, Inc., 1992.

Rahner, Karl, S.J. *Bishops: Their Status and Function*. Baltimore: Helicon Press, 1964.

_____. "Christianity as Church." Chap. in *Foundations of Christian Faith: An Introduction to the Idea of Christianity*. Translated by William V. Dych. New York: Crossroad, 1992.

Rahner, Karl, S.J., ed. *Encyclopedia of Theology: A Concise Sacramentum Mundi.* New York: The Seabury Press, 1975. S.v. "Apostolic Succession" by Wilhelm Breuning, and "Orders and Ordination" by Piet Franzen.

Rahner, Karl, S.J. and Herbert Vorgrimler. *Theological Dictionary.* Edited by Cornelius Ernst, O.P. Translated by Richard Strachan. New York: Herder & Herder, 1965. S.v. "Apostolic Succession."

Ratzinger, Joseph Cardinal. *Principles of Catholic Theology. Building Stones for a Fundamental Theology.* Translated by Sister Mary Frances McCarthy, S.N.D. San Francisco: Ignatius Press, 1987.

Sharkey, Michael, ed. *International Theological Commission: Texts and Documents.* 1969-1985. With a Foreword by Joseph Cardinal Ratzinger. San Francisco: Ignatius Press, 1989.

Sullivan, Francis A., S.J. *The Church We Believe In: One, Holy, Catholic and Apostolic.* New York: Paulist Press, 1988.

Thurian, Max, ed. *Churches Respond to "Baptism, Eucharist and Ministry" I.* Geneva: WCC (coll. Faith and Order Paper No. 144), 1988.

Tillard, J.M.R., O.P. "Recognition of ministries: What is the real problem?" *One in Christ* 21 (1985): 31-39.

Torrance, Thomas F. "Memoranda on Orthodox/Reformed Relations." Chap. in *Theological Dialogue between Orthodox and Reformed Churches*, ed. Thomas F. Torrance. Edinburgh/London: Scottish Academic Press, 1985.

*Unity We Seek, The. A Statement by the Roman Catholic/Presbyterian-Reformed Consultation.* Edited by Bishop Ernest L. Unterkoefler and Dr. Andrew Harsanyi. New York: Paulist Press, 1977.

*Universal Jewish Encyclopedia*, 1948 ed. S.v. "Ordination."

Villain, Maurice, S.M. "Can There Be Apostolic Succession outside the Chain of Imposition of Hands?" *Concilium.* Vol. 34, *Apostolic Succession: Rethinking a Barrier to Unity*, ed. Hans Küng. New York: Paulist Press, 1968.

Von Allmen, Jean-Jacques. "Ordination — A Sacrament? A Protestant Reply." *Concilium.* Vol. 74, *The Plurality of*

*Ministries*, ed. Hans Küng and Walter Kasper. New York: Herder & Herder, 1972.

Von Campenhausen, Hans. *Ecclesiastical Authority and Spiritual Power in the Church of the First Three Centuries.* Translated by J.A. Baker. Palo Alto, CA: Stanford University Press, 1969.

Vorgrimler, Herbert. *Sacramental Theology.* Translated by Linda M. Maloney. Collegeville, MN: Liturgical Press, 1992.

Ware, Kallistos (Timothy). *The Orthodox Church.* Rev. ed. New York: Viking Penguin, 1983.

World Council of Churches. *Baptism, Eucharist and Ministry, 1982-1990. Report on the Processes and Responses.* Geneva: WCC (coll. Faith and Order Paper No. 149), 1992.

World Council of Churches/Roman Catholic Joint Theological Commission on "Catholicity and Apostolicity." "Study Document." *One in Christ* 6 (1970): 452-83.